What People Are Saying About

Everything You Wanted To Know About Credit

"I give Renee & Anthony's book a 5-star rating. This book should be required reading for everyone from the age of 13 and up. It's a great example of the kind of book that we should have in schools as part of a desperately needed financial literacy curriculum."
— Alfred A. Edmond Jr., Sr. VP/Editor-in-Chief, BLACK ENTERPRISE

"Renee D. Crenshaw has created a very clearly written book that easily guides the reader through important credit information. I highly recommend this book."
— Garrett Sutton Esq., Rich Dad's Advisor, author of "The ABC's of Getting Out of Debt" and founder of Success DNA

"I highly recommend *Everything You Ever Wanted to Know About Credit but Were Ashamed to Ask*. This book gives a thorough overview of credit and is written in a style that's easy to understand and follow. It helps you understand your credit score and provides practical guidance on how to repair your credit on your own."
— Shelly A. Anthony, Philadelphia Community Development Officer, Wachovia Corporation

"This book is very innovative and a powerful resource for everyone who wants to improve their finances and credit standing."
— Honorable Jewell Williams, House of Representatives, 197th Legislative District

"Renee and Anthony's Everything You Wanted To Know About Credit is like American Express You Can't Leave Home Without It."
— Minister Eugene Coleman, Beloved St. John Evangelistic Church

"People are drastically affected by their lack of knowledge of credit and debt. This book is one of the best financial literacy tools I've ever seen. We recommend it to all my clients."
— Charles D. Williams, President, Conestoga Mortgage

What People Are Saying About

Renee D. Crenshaw & Anthony B. Miles

"Anthony B. Miles has great vision, courage and insight. His love for the community is such that he wants more for them than they want for themselves. He wants to awaken people to themselves, and to an instant future of abundance. I congratulate, honor and encourage him to keep on doing this noble task."
— Mark Victor Hansen, Co-creator of the best-selling "Chicken Soup for the Soul" series and co-author of "The One-Minute Millionaire"

"Your names will become synonymous with the economic empowerment of the African American community. You, however, have broken the barrier that so many have failed to break. The barrier of consideration and uncertainty. You have taken massive action. And massive action creates massive results. I am honored to be part of your team. Anything you need…let me know and you've got it."
— Blair Singer, Rich Dad's Advisor and author of "Sales Dogs"

"You've created something that is destined to grow and expand based on your leadership. I congratulate you on your efforts and the results you achieved. It's great to be apart of something new and exciting."
— Robert Stuberg, author of "The 12 Wealth Secrets"

EVERYTHING YOU WANTED TO KNOW ABOUT CREDIT BUT WERE TOO ASHAMED TO ASK

Renee D. Crenshaw and Anthony B. Miles

Rising Star Foundation, Philadelphia, Pennsylvania

Everything You Wanted to Know About Credit But Were Too Ashamed To Ask

Tools, Tips and Hidden Secrets to Fixing Bad Credit, Building and Maintaining AAA Credit

By Renee D. Crenshaw
and Anthony B. Miles

Library of Congress Control Number: 2004099545

ISBN 0-9747086-1-5 (paperback)

Published in The United States of America by:
Rising Star Foundation
633 N. 33rd Street, 1st Floor
Philadelphia, PA 19104 U.S.A.

Cover design by Josh Laird
Cover copyrighting by Anthony B. Miles & Renee D. Crenshaw
Book interior design by KrisBp Design

GIVING BACK:

A PORTION OF THE PROCEEDS FROM THIS BOOK BENEFIT CHARITY

Renee D. Crenshaw and Anthony B. Miles will designate one or more charities to receive a portion of the profits from each book from their "Everything You Wanted To Know About" book series. A portion of the proceeds from Everything You Wanted To Know About Credit will be donated to the Rising Star Foundation and National Personal Finance Makeover Fund: A fund that makes the dream of financial independence a reality for people less fortunate.

For more information about Rising Star Foundation or the National Personal Finance Makeover Fund contact us at (215) 222-0390.

ACKNOWLEDGMENTS

Special thanks to Anthony Miles and Clinton Bush for believing in this work and for touching and agreeing with me in prayer for its manifestation. In Isaiah 54:2, God says: ***"Enlarge the place of your tent, and let back the curtains of your habitations: Spare not, lengthen your cords, and strengthen your stakes; for you shall break forth on the right hand and on the left; and your descendants shall possess the nations and restore the desolate cities."*** *Because you have been faithful over a few things, I pray that God will make you rulers of much.*

Jenell Fritz you have proved to be a great friend to me and a wonderful Godmother to my child. You were very instrumental in my completion of this work. You prayed with me. You watched my child for me while I worked. There is so much Godly wisdom and discernment in you. Thank you for restoring me back to the fold, through prayer and love. Never once did you judge me or show me any unkindness. I pray that whenever you leave this world, you will leave empty, having released into the Earth everything that God has deposited in you.

To my uncles and aunts, Henry, Eugene, Betty and Rita Pearson, thank you for your love and support over the years. It is greatly appreciated. May the blessings of the Lord be poured out upon you and His goodness and mercy follow you all the days of your lives.

DEDICATION

This guide is dedicated to the memory of those who fought and died so that I might have the right to the pursuit of happiness by fulfilling my God-given purpose.

It is dedicated to the slaves who lost their freedom but never gave up on life and hope. What you did so that I might live and be free, was not done in vain.

I dedicate this work also to those in my family who have gone on and are not here to witness their influence on my life. May you all rest in peace.

I dedicate this work to my family and friends who believed in me, and also to those folks who didn't believe in me, you have both inspired me to be my best.

I dedicate this work to my daughter. Monet Noel, Mommy loves you.

Last and certainly not least, this work is dedicated to the creator of all things, my Lord Jesus Christ, without his inspiration, impartation, and motivation, I could not have completed this product. Father you have been so good to me and I thank you for what you've done in my life and the things that are yet to come. I am truly grateful.

DISCLAIMER

While all attempts were made to verify information, the authors do not assume any responsibility for errors, inaccuracies or omissions. Although it is the authors' desire to distribute useful information to the public in the most complete manner, they are not attorneys, a collection agency or bankers and any slight of people or organizations is unintentional. No warranties of any kind are made of any kind with regard to the completeness or accuracy of this book.

The reader of this publication assumes responsibility for the use of this information. Before you rely on any of the information contained in this book you are advised to retain competent counsel to determine what state and/or federal laws or regulations may apply to the reader's particular situation. The author assumes no responsibility or liability whatsoever on behalf of any purchaser or reader of these materials.

This material relates to laws and customs in the United States and should not be used as a guide to consumer credit in other countries. Every effort has been made to make this an informative and useful credit manual.

TABLE OF CONTENTS

ABOUT THE AUTHORS

Renee D. Crenshaw

Anthony B. Miles

Renee D. Crenshaw and Anthony B. Miles are America's leading authorities on urban personal finance. Over the past 8 years, Renee D. Crenshaw and Anthony B. Miles have empowered thousands of individuals to "Take Control of their Finances". As prolific teachers, Anthony & Renee has written and published numerous articles, special reports and books. Their latest work, Everything You Wanted To Know About Real Estate Investing But Didn't Know Whom To Ask and Everything You Wanted To Know About Getting Out of Debt and Reaching Your Financial Goals are scheduled to be released in mid 2005.

INTRODUCTION

The purpose of this guide is to provide you with the tools to get a handle on your credit and to help you take control of your financial future. With the information contained in this guide, if applied properly you can experience immediate results in restoring your credit.

However, please understand that this is not a credit repair guide per se. If you have poor credit because you are irresponsible with money and paying your bills, this guide will not help you. If on the other hand, circumstances have happened in your life to cause some misfortune or you are simply not knowledgeable about credit matters, this guide will definitely be a valuable resource.

The guide consists of a number of frequently asked questions along with some interesting tips, and well-kept secrets about credit restoration. The first section is dedicated to giving you an understanding of how the credit industry operates and how it effects your credit standing. The latter portion of the book provides you with suggestions and tips for credit management.

It is hoped at the conclusion of this guide you will feel more confident in your ability to manage your credit and you will learn to avoid all of the land mines and booby traps that will destroy your credit.

SHARE WITH US

We would love to hear your reactions to our credit resource guide. Please let us know which sections were the most valuable and how you used them to improve your credit. Write us and send your testimonies to:

Everything You Wanted to Know About Credit
Attn: Renee D. Crenshaw and Anthony B. Miles
643 N. 33rd Street, 1st Floor
Philadelphia, PA 19104

CREDIT BUREAUS

Did you know that credit bureaus receive most of your personal information from creditors when you apply for credit?

The creditor shares the information with the credit bureaus, who in turn use the information to update your credit file.

CREDIT BUREAUS

How do credit bureaus get my credit information?

Credit Bureaus get consumer credit information from such institutions as banks, savings and loans, credit card companies, and other types of financial institutions. These suppliers of your credit information are called automatic subscribers. When you complete an application for credit, including a mortgage, cell phone, insurance, etc., the subscriber shares this information with the credit bureau, who in turn adds this information to your credit file. For instance, if you provide a different address than what is already in your file, that information will be added to your file as your most current address. In exchange for providing the credit bureaus with this information, the subscribers receive discount rates for credit reports of their potentially new clients.

Some creditors, such as insurance agencies, utility companies, cable companies and medical facilities report only when payments are severely overdue, in which case a collection agency is hired or legal action taken.

The FLOW of CREDIT INFORMATION

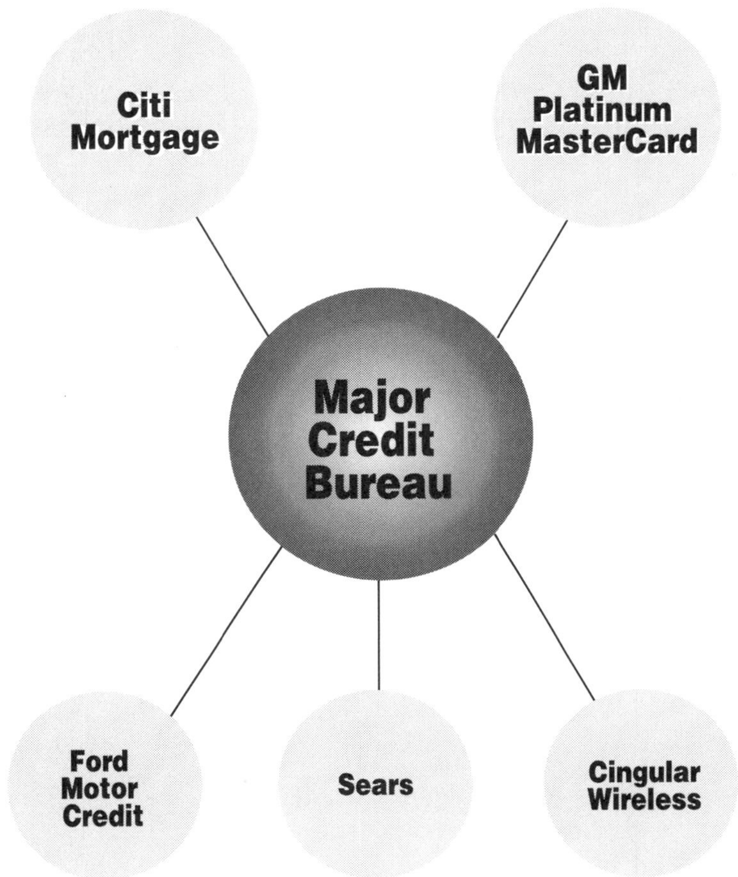

- **The credit bureaus receive information about you from your lenders and potential lenders.** These lenders have agreements with the credit bureau to provide information about you during the duration of your loan.
- **Your lender passes on information concerning:** late payments, balances, etc.
- **The credit bureau(s) add this information to your credit file.**
- **The credit bureaus then sell the information they have in your credit file to other credit grantors who wish to review your history before they lend you money.** The credit bureaus also sell your information to others who may be interested in prequalifying you for pre-approved credit offers. Which would explain why you receive unsolicited pre-approval offers from companies you haven't sought for credit.

Are credit bureaus connected to the Federal Government?

NO.

Credit Bureaus have no legal power over you, and since the bureaus have made so many errors in the past, Federal Laws regarding credit information are very much in your favor.

?

Did You Know?

Credit Counseling Services get paid by your creditors. Usually creditors give 10% of your payments back to those agencies.

Why are there major differences in the information contained in my credit file from all three major credit reporting agencies?

Although, the major credit reporting agencies maintain a credit file on you, they are competitors and do not share information. Differences occur when creditors report to only one or two of the three bureaus.

Also, each credit agency has it own method for updating credit files. As a result, incorrect or outdated information may not be removed from your file for all three agencies at the same time or at all for that matter. That's why it is so important for you to review all three credit reports, side-by-side at least once every 90-days, so that you may clear up any errors that are listed on your reports.

It is important to remember that almost everything in your credit file is used to provide your creditor with a credit score, which is used heavily to determine the interest you will pay for your next loan.

Did You Know?

Opening several credit accounts in a short period of time, could have a negative effect on your credit. Research shows that opening several credit accounts in a short period of time, represents greater risk, especially for people who do not have a long-established credit history. Therefore, you may want to think twice about opening multiple lines of credit at one time.

Who Are The Major Credit Bureaus?

There are actually three major credit bureaus, Experian, Equifax, Inc. and Trans Union Corporation. Although your creditor may pull a copy of your report from a small unknown credit bureau, in all likelihood the smaller bureau is getting your credit information from the major credit bureaus. There are, in fact, over 1000 local and regional credit bureaus throughout the United States. **The 3 Major Credit Bureaus are often referred to as the Big Three.** These major credit bureaus are competitors, which means each company has a different version of your credit history.

NEED TO CONTACT THE BIG 3?

Equifax, Inc.
P.O. Box 740241
Atlanta, GA 30374
(800) 685-1111
www.equifax.com

Trans Union Corp.
P.O. Box 1000
Chester, PA 19022
(800) 888-4213
www.transunion.com

Experian
P.O. Box 2002
Allen, TX 75013
(888) 397-3742
www.experian.com

A FORTH MAJOR CREDIT BUREAU?

Although kept very quiet, there is another credit reporting bureau on the scene. Innovis Data Solutions is in the business of collecting your personal credit information. However, Innovis does not sell consumer credit reports, to creditors, insurers or potential employers. This new credit reporting agency gathers your credit information and sells it to companies that compile mailing lists for unsolicited credit offers.

Although the information Innovis provides to creditors is not used to deny you credit, insurance or employment, it is used for marketing purposes, and Innovis report consumers who are a high credit risk. For example, Innovis offers a product called Filesafe to its customers. Filesafe is a database that contains derogatory information about consumers, such as late payments. The company listed the following statement on their website.

"You can cleanse your pre-approved mailing lists before offers are printed and mailed... reducing cost and risk... One last screening against FileSafe will safely eliminate the undesirable names prior to your mail date."

Another product that Innovis offers is New Movers, which provides on a monthly basis updated change of address information for consumers.

The following statement was found on the Fannie Mae website for their lenders:

"Each month you must notify the four major credit repositories of the status of loans you service for Fannie Mae... This requires you to provide a "full-file status report as of the last day of each month."

Fannie Mae, a financial corporation that provides mortgage funds to lenders, includes Innovis in their list of the major credit repositories to which lenders should report. Also, when calling the toll-free "opt-out" number (which is used to remove your name from lists that credit bureaus sell to telemarketers and creditors) Innovis, Experian, Equifax and TransUnion are listed as the credit reporting agencies that will remove your name from their list.

Another interesting finding is that Sallie Mae, the largest provider of student loans, has discontinued its reporting to Experian and Trans Union. Instead, they are reporting to Innovis and Equifax. This is not good news for students with Sallie Mae student loans. Those in good standing with their student loans will not reap the benefits of being a good borrower because their credit history is not being reported to all three of the major credit bureaus. When these students graduate and decide to purchase their first home, if they are in good standing, not having these student loans listed on their credit report could significantly affect them during the mortgage evaluation process.

Mortgage lenders usually pull a 3-in-1 credit report to evaluate your credit. These reports consist of information from Experian, Equifax and Trans Union. The lender will use the middle score from the three bureaus to determine if an applicant will be approved for a mortgage and at what interest rate the mortgage will be offered.

If Sallie Mae no longer reports to Experian and Trans Union, the consumer's credit file for both bureaus will be missing positive payment information used to calculate the consumer's credit score. Since lenders use the middle credit score to determine interest rate and credit approval, Sallie Mae's failure to report the consumer's good payment history to two of the major credit bureaus could hurt the mortgage applicant.

To obtain a copy of your Innovis credit report, put your request in writing and include the following:

- Full Name
- Current Address (along with a utility bill showing your current address)
- Previous addresses for the past 2 years
- Social Security Number
- Date of Birth
- Current Employer
- Phone Number
- Signature

Mail your request to:
Innovis Consumer Assistance
P.O. Box 1358
Columbus, OH 43216-1358

Send a check or money order:

California	**$8.00**
Minnesota	**$8.00**
Montana	**$8.00**
Colorado	**Free (First Report)**
Connecticut	**Free (First Report)**
Georgia	**Free (First Report)**
Maine	**Free (First Report)**
Maryland	**Free (First Report)**
Massachusetts	**Free (First Report)**
New Jersey	**Free (First Report)**
Vermont	**Free (First Report)**
All other States	**$8.00**

You may reach Innovis by telephone at: 1-800-540-2505 or visit the website at www.innovis.com.

When communicating with the credit bureaus, how much information should I provide?

No more than what is necessary. Never, ever give the credit bureau more information than is needed to investigate your dispute. The bureaus have a right to request a copy of your social security card. However, do not send them a copy of your driver's license. Never forget that the bureaus are in the business of collecting information about you and selling it to not only your creditors, but also to other customers like telemarketing companies for solicitation purposes.

DID YOU KNOW...

If you are denied credit due to information contained in your credit file, the provider is required by Section 615(a) of the Fair Credit Reporting Act to notify you. The notification may be done in writing, orally, or by electronic means.

The notification must include the following:

- The name, address, and telephone number of the Credit reporting agency.
- A statement indicating that the credit reporting agency did not make the adverse decision and is unable to explain why the decision was made.
- Notification to the consumer of their right to obtain a free credit report, if requested within 60 days, from the credit reporting agency that supplied the information.
- Information regarding the consumer's right to dispute directly with the credit reporting agency the accuracy or completeness of any information provided by the credit reporting agency.

Did You Know?

Cleaning up your credit report with one of the major bureaus does not mean that you won't have to do the same with the other two.

The bureaus are competitors and do not share your credit file information

What laws are in place to protect me and my credit?

There are a number of laws in place to protect you from unfair and deceptive credit practices, eight are listed below.

1. Fair Debt Collection Practices Act

Prohibits debt collectors from engaging in abusive, dishonest and under handed methods for collecting debts. Under this act, collectors must provide you with a written notice which includes the name of the creditor, and the amount owed. According to this law, collectors can call you only between the hours of 8 am and 9 pm, and when they call, must identify themselves.

2. Equal Credit Opportunity Act

Prohibits discrimination on the basis of sex, race, marital status, religion, national origin, age or receipt of public assistance, such as social security or disability benefits. Ensures that all have the right to obtain credit. It is illegal for a lender to refuse to consider income because it comes from child support, alimony, part-time employment, or retirement benefits.

3. Truth in Lending Act

Mandates disclosure of information regarding the cost of credit. All costs of a loan offer, including finance charges and the annual percentage rate, must be displayed prominently on forms and statements used by creditors. It also protects you against unauthorized use of your credit card. If your card is lost or stolen and you report it, the most you will be responsible for is $50.

4. Fair Credit and Charge Card Disclosure Act

This act is a provision within the Truth in Lending Act that requires a box be placed on credit card applications that describes a credit card's key features and costs including, the annual percentage rate, grace period for purchases, minimum finance charge, balance calculation method, annual fees, transaction fees for cash advances, and penalty fees such as over-the-limit fees and late-payment fees.

5. Consumer Credit Reporting Reform Act

This act is an amendment to the Fair Credit Reporting Act, which requires credit bureaus to notify consumers before reinstating information that was deleted from their credit file. Also, the act mandates free credit reports for the unemployed, persons on public assistance, and fraud victims. Credit Reporting Agencies are required to list the full trade name of those requesting a credit report within the past year and share corrections among credit bureaus through an automated system. It also addresses the time limit for the reporting of information in your credit file.

6. Credit Repair Organizations Act

Makes it illegal for credit counselors to advise consumers to make untrue statements to dispute accurate, negative information or to alter or hide their identity to remove or hide negative credit information. Credit repair organizations must provide consumers with a summary of rights under federal and state credit laws and a dated, written contract, which can be canceled within three business days.

7. Fair Credit Reporting Act

Instructs credit reporting agencies to furnish credit reports only to those who have a permissible purpose for the information, and requires credit reporting agencies to remove obsolete information from credit reports. It gives you the right to know what is in your credit report and requires that both credit bureaus and information providers, such as a credit card company, have an obligation to correct mistakes made to your credit file. You have the right to dispute inaccurate information and to know which credit bureau provided a report when you are denied credit.

8. Fair Credit Billing Act

Addresses credit card billing problems and covers all open-end credit accounts (such as department store cards and overdraft checking). The act provides a step-by-step procedure to resolve billing errors. The procedure is as follows:

- You should send a written notice of a billing error within 60 days of receiving the first bill containing an error.

- The creditor must acknowledge the notice within 30 days and resolve the dispute within two billing cycles, but not longer than 90 days.

- Within 90 days, the creditor must explain why the bill is correct or correct the error, and no collection activity is permitted or finance charges assessed for the amount in question while the item is being disputed.

- If upon receiving the findings of the investigation, you believe the billing is still in error, you must notify the creditor in writing. Please note, however that at this point, if it is found that you owe the amount in question, and you do not pay it, the creditor may now report you as delinquent, but they must also report that the amount is in dispute.

Do Credit Bureaus profit from maintaining my credit information?

Credit information gathering and reporting is a big money making business. Like other commercial businesses, credit bureaus are in this business to make a profit. They make their money selling your private and personal information to their clients; which include, creditors, employers, landlords, mortgage companies, insurers, telemarketing and mailing list companies, just to name a few. According to the Associated Credit Bureaus, which is a credit industry organization, over three million credit reports are issued each business day in the U.S. With the average cost of a credit report being around $8.50, the credit industry is making at least $25 million dollars a day on the sale of credit reports alone.

PROTECT YOUR PRIVACY "OPT OUT"

Stop the credit bureaus from selling your personal credit information to telemarketers and creditors without your permission. OPT-OUT NOW.

To remove your name from lists sold by the National Credit Bureaus, "Opt-out." Call 1-888-5-OPT-OUT (567-8688) and when the message starts, choose option #2 and then option #3, which will remove your name from the list forever.

Immediately upon receipt of your message, it is sent to Experian, Equifax, TransUnion and Innovis, and posted to your credit file. You should receive confirmation of your "opting out" within a week after making the call.

IT'S THE LAW!

Consumer credit transactions are regulated both at the Federal and the State level. Some of the Federal laws influencing the credit industry are:

Truth in Lending Act
Fair Credit and Charge Card Disclosure Act
Fair Credit Reporting Act
Equal Credit Opportunity Act
Fair Credit Billing Act
Right to Financial Privacy Act
Consumer Leasing Act
Fair Debt Collection Practices Act

LETTER RECEIVED AFTER OPTING-OUT

After you call to Opt-out, you will receive a letter similar to the one listed below - that must be completed and returned to finalize the process.

- **EQUIFAX**
- **EXPERIAN**
- **INNOVIS**
- **TRANS UNION**

Renee D. Crenshaw
1234 Prosperity Lane
Righteousness, KOG

This letter is in response to your request, and in accordance with the Fair Credit Reporting Act, to be permanently excluded from all pre-approved credit offer mailing lists by credit grantors utilizing EQUIFAX, EXPERIAN, INNOVIS, OR TRANS UNION databases. However, you may continue to get marketing materials from companies who do not use consumer data to compile lists.

- **The personal information that you provide is confidential and will be used only to process your request. Failure to provide complete accurate information may prevent or delay the processing of your request.**
- **Please check this box if the name and address above are correct. Sign and date below and return to the address listed below.**

Please check this box if the name and address above are incorrect.
Make any necessary changes below, sign and date and return to the address listed below.......

A Summary of Your Rights Under the Fair Credit Reporting Act

The federal Fair Credit Reporting Act (FCRA) is designed to promote accuracy, fairness, and privacy of information in the files of every credit bureau.

The FCRA gives you specific rights, as outlined below.

- **You must be told if information in your file has been used to deny you credit or against you in some other manner.** Anyone who uses information from a credit reporting agency to take action against you must tell you, and give you the name, address, and phone number of the credit reporting agencies that provided the consumer reports.

- **You may have access to your credit file.** Upon your request, a credit reporting agency must provide you with a copy of your credit report. If you have been turned down for credit or some other adverse action has been taken due to what is contained in your credit file, the credit bureau that provided the information is required to provide you with a free copy of your report if you make the request within 60 days of receiving notice of the action.

- **You can dispute inaccurate information with the credit reporting agencies.** If you advise a credit reporting agency that your credit report contains inaccurate information, they must investigate the items (usually within 30 days) by presenting to its information source all relevant evidence you provide.

- **You must receive a written report from the credit reporting agency upon the conclusion of the investigation.** Also a copy of your report must be sent to you if any changes are made to your file as a result of the investigation. If an item is deleted or a dispute statement is filed, you may request that anyone who has recently received your report be notified of the change.

- **Inaccurate information must be corrected or deleted.** A credit reporting agency must remove inaccurate or unverified information from its files. The credit reporting agency is not required to remove accurate information unless it is outdated or is not verified.

- **You must be notified by the credit reporting agency if they reinsert information into your credit file.** If you dispute an item on your credit report and it is removed, but some time later the sources do verify, the information can be reinserted into your credit file.

- **You can dispute inaccurate items with the source of the information.** In addition, once you notify the source of the error in writing, it may not continue to report the information if it is an error.

- **Outdated information may not be reported.** In most cases this means any information over 7 years.

- **Access to your file is restricted to those who have a legitimate business need.** A credit reporting agency may provide information about you to those with a need recognized by the FCRA — usually to consider an application with a creditor, insurer, employer, landlord, or other business.

- **Your consent is required for reports that contain medical information.** Credit reporting agencies may not share medical information about you to creditors, insurers, or employers without your permission.

- **You may have your name removed from credit reporting agency lists for unsolicited credit and insurance offers.** If you decide to remove your name from the list, you may call 1-888-5-OPT-OUT. You will be sent a form that must be completed and returned to remove you from lists of the four major credit reporting agencies.

- **You may seek damages from violators.** If a credit reporting agency violates the Fair Credit Reporting Act, you may sue them.

What kind of information do credit bureaus gather on me?

Credit Bureaus collect financial and other personal information about you to compile and maintain your credit file for the purpose of providing you, a current creditor or potential creditor, with your personal credit history. **The credit bureaus gather the following information to place into your credit file:**

Consumer Identifying Information

- Name
- Social Security Number
- Date of Birth
- Former Names or Aliases
- Current and Former Addresses
- Employer
- Profession
- Telephone Number

Public Records

- Civil Judgments
- Tax Lien
- Bankruptcies
- Foreclosures
- Delinquent Child Support payments
- Wage garnishment
- Financial counseling Information

Collection Accounts

- Collections Agency Name
- Date Collection Account Opened
- Last date updated by Collections Agency
- The amount placed for collection
- Outstanding Balance
- Name of original creditor

Credit Accounts

- Date the account was opened
- Date of last activity
- Past due accounts
- Credit limit on each account
- Type of loan account (revolving, installment, line of credit, mortgage, etc)
- Highest Balance or amount ever owed by borrower
- Credit limit on the account
- Balance due
- Payment size
- Past due amount
- Payment pattern for the last 12-24 months
- Number of times account was late by 30, 60, or 90 days.
- Numerical Code for payment method
  (code indicates the account is current, late or in collections).

Credit Inquiries

- List of companies who have requested consumer credit information
- Date the inquiries were made

Do Credit Bureaus rate my credit?

No, credit bureaus do not rate credit, approve or reject consumer applications for credit. The credit bureau provides a snapshot of your current credit profile to creditors to assist them in making their decision to grant or deny you credit. The information that the credit bureau provides consists of your total credit file and a three digit credit score which represents a summation of risk of repayment of debt.

To provide the creditor with a score, your credit file is ranked against all other consumers with credit within the credit bureau's individual credit repository. Thus, the credit score that Experian provides would be a result of comparing your credit file to others within it's own (Experian) repository.

MAKING LOTS OF MONEY EVERYDAY

All three of the major credit reporting agencies, Experian, Equifax and Trans Union, on an average day process over 3 billion pieces of information from creditors and issue more than 3 million credit reports each business day.

Why would I have bad credit if I never have used credit?

Everyone has a credit rating even if you have never had a credit card or a loan. In the eyes of lenders, a person with no credit activity in their credit file is considered to be almost as much of a risk as somebody with bad credit.

The bottom line is, without a credit activity in their credit file you are considered a big credit risk and your credit score will suffer greatly. Listed below are a few reasons why your credit score might be low as a result of having little to no credit activity in your credit file.

- **Account payment or credit history not long enough**
- **Lack of recent information on accounts**
- **Insufficient number of satisfactory accounts**
- **Too few or no recent balances on revolving accounts** *(e.g. credit cards)*

Did You Know?

You do not have to provide permission for a company or another person to obtain your credit report if they have a permissible business purpose for pulling your credit report, which could include pre-approved credit solicitations and telemarketing.

Did You Know?

American Express charge cards have little affect on your credit score while American Express credit cards carry the same weight as major bank credit cards such as VISA and MasterCard.

DID YOU KNOW?

Credit counseling won't hurt your credit score because the FICO formula no longer includes this information in your credit score calculations. But your creditors may report to the credit bureaus that your account is included in a credit counseling program which will be noted in your credit file. Also, your lender may report you as late, because you are not paying what was originally agreed upon, and/or because the credit counselor isn't sending your payments in on time. To avoid ruining your credit because of late payments, make sure that the credit counseling company is making your payments on time.

CREDIT REPORTS

Everyone has one, what is yours saying about you?

CREDIT REPORTS

What is the purpose of a credit report?

A credit report is a record of how you manage your credit obligations. The purpose of the credit report is to give your lender, potential lenders, employers or any person who pulls your credit report an accounting of how you pay and have paid your debts, the level of debt you have carried and are currently carrying and the type of debt you have had and currently have.

What information can be found in my credit report?

A credit report consists of 4 major parts:

1. Personal

This section contains your name, previous names, date of birth, Social Security Number, address, previous address, employer, previous employer, spouse, previous spouse, and home telephone number.

2. Public Record

In this section can be found any derogatory public record information that is readily accessible to the public such as bankruptcies, federal or state tax liens, wage garnishments, civil judgments, orders to pay child support, felony convictions, etc.

3. Credit History

The credit history portion of your credit report consists of two parts - Credit Accounts and Collection Accounts.

a. Credit Accounts

This section provides a snapshot of the credit status of your revolving and installment loans, which includes credit cards and automobile loans and leases. Mortgage loans and collection accounts can be found in this section as well. All credit account information is listed including your positive and negative account activity.

b. Collection Accounts

When your credit account is referred to a collection agency for debt collection, it will appear in this section of your report. Regardless of whether it appears on the report as a paid or unpaid collection, this derogatory mark on your credit report is considered by most creditors as very negative.

4. Inquiries

Anyone who has requested your credit report will be listed in this section. Creditors, insurance companies, collection agencies, potential employers, the IRS or anyone else who pulls your credit report will be listed in this section by name and the date they pulled your report. Too many inquiries listed on your credit report within a short period of time will raise a red flag with some creditors and may result in you being denied credit.

How long must derogatory marks remain on my credit report?

There is no law or statue that instructs credit bureaus and creditors to keep negative information on your credit report.

The Fair Credit Reporting Act (FCRA), provides a limit on how long negative information can remain on your credit report. Many people believe that their creditor, by law, must report a derogatory mark for a proscribed period of time. This is absolutely false. Your creditor may at any time instruct the credit bureau to remove negative information from your credit file. The law basically protects the consumer from being penalized indefinitely for a derogatory mark in their credit file. However, there are some exceptions.

The following credit report entries could remain on your report indefinitely.

- Unpaid tax liens
- Information about criminal convictions
- Information in response to an application for a job with a salary of more than $75,000
- Information reported because of an application for more than $150,000 worth of credit or life insurance

When Must It Come Off?

(Remember whoever reports it, can request it come off at anytime)

Late Payments

Creditors may report your account as late when you are **30** to **180** days past due. These negative marks must be removed from your credit report **7** years from the date of the late payment.

Child Support Judgments

These judgments must be removed from your credit report **7** years from the date when the judgment was filed.

Collection Accounts

Must be removed **7** years from the date of the initial missed payment that led to the collection. If you pay-off the collection account within the **7** year period, the account will be marked "paid collection" on your credit report. However, it will still be viewed and scored as a negative mark. Also, paying off the collection will not re-age your account. In other words, it will not restart the 7 year clock.

Closed or Inactive Accounts

Closed Accounts are those that are no longer available for use.
Accounts closed by the grantor are considered negative and will remain on your credit report for up to **7** years. A closed account may or may not have an account balance and if the account has derogatory marks, those delinquencies must be removed **7** years from the date they are reported. Accounts closed without any delinquencies will remain on your credit report for up to **10** years.

Charged-off Accounts

Must be removed **7** years from the date of the initial missed payment. The account can not be re-aged if you make payments after the account has been charged-off.

Lost Credit Card

Normally, a lost credit card account will remain on your credit report for **2** years from the date that the card was reported lost. However if there are derogatory marks showing on the account, they will be reported for **7** years.

Civil Suits and Judgments

Civil Suits, judgments and records of arrest must be removed from your credit report within **7** years from the date it was reported or until the governing statute of limitations has expired, whichever is the longer period.

Tax Liens

Outstanding taxes may remain on your credit report indefinitely.

Paid Liens

Paid liens remain **7** years from the paid date of the lien.

Inquiries

Inquiries will remain on your credit report for **2** years. Although there are two kinds of inquiries listed on your report, hard (inquiries resulting from you pursuing some form of credit) and soft inquiries (inquiries resulting from employment and pre-approval offers of credit), only the hard inquiries negatively effect your credit report.

Criminal Conviction

May be reported on your credit report indefinitely.

Bankruptcy

There are three different types of bankruptcy filings that may effect your credit. Bankruptcy is reported for **10** years from the date the bankruptcy is discharged or from the date the bankruptcy case is adjudicated. *(See examples below of how long bankruptcies may be reported on your credit report.)*

Chapter 7

You file bankruptcy on May 1, 2003 and receive a discharge on October 31, 2003. The bankruptcy will remain on your credit report for **10** years from the date of discharge, that would be October 2013.

Chapter 11

You file bankruptcy on May 1, 2003. You receive confirmation of your Chapter 11 Plan on August 1, 2003. The bankruptcy remains on your credit report for **10** years from the date that your Chapter 11 Plan was confirmed, which according to this example would be August 2013.

Chapter 12 and 13

You file bankruptcy on May 1, 2003. On October 1, 2006, the court grants you a discharge after you complete all payments under your 3 year repayment plan. In this case, the bankruptcy remains on your credit for **10** years from your discharge on October 1, 2006.

Any credit accounts included in the bankruptcy must be removed **7** years from the date they were reported as included in the bankruptcy.

Positive Credit Accounts

Positive open credit files may remain indefinitely on your credit report. Paid positive closed accounts remain for 10 years.

The TOP CREDIT REPORT KILLERS

- **Bankruptcy**
- **Foreclosure**
- **Repossession**
- **Charge-Offs**
- **Collections**
- **Court Judgments**
- **IRS Liens**
- **120 days late payment**
- **90 days late payment**
- **30 days late payment**
- **Too Many Credit Inquiries**

Listed from the most severe to the least severe

What are the negative marks that could show up on my credit report?

When reviewing your application for credit, lenders will look for negative entries. These negative entries are viewed as red flags and if not severe enough to deny you credit, the lender may require you to provide a written explanation before granting you credit.

Always remember that it is in the lender's best interest to identify any area of risk that may effect your ability to repay the loan as agreed. No one is willing to grant you credit if they believe you will default.

Here are some of the red Flags that creditors look for and how they, (whether true or not) may interpret them:

- **Bankruptcy** — you once were financially irresponsible and/or unable to pay your obligations as agreed.

- **Child Support** — you did not pay your court ordered child support payments as ordered. Appears to be irresponsible in taking care of your children and have little regard for the law.

- **Court Judgments** — there is a judgment on record against you due to losing a lawsuit. Creditors may want to know why you lost the lawsuit, if you were at fault and how it may effect your ability to repay your loan.

- **Charge-Off** — the creditor could not collect the debt from you and will assume the loss by writing it off and claim the loss for tax purposes. It appears that you were unresponsive to the collection action made by the creditor to get you to pay off the debt.

- **Paid Charge-Off** — you paid off the debt after the creditor wrote it off as a loss. Although you paid off the account it may remain on your report as a negative mark for up to 7 years and will have a negative impact on your credit score.

- **IRS Liens** — you owe the IRS taxes and a lien has been placed against your property until what is owed is paid. The creditor could see this as your inability to pay your current government debt. Upon payment in full of this debt, the negative mark may remain on your credit report for another 7 years.

- **Collections** — as a result of your creditor's unsuccessful attempt to collect payment from you, they had to refer the account to a collection agency to try to get you to pay your outstanding debt.

- **Paid Collections** — a collection agency was successful in getting you to pay a debt that their client, your creditor, could not.

- **Repossession** — the taking back of property by a creditor from the borrower, due to you not paying your bill.

- **Tax Lien** — you owe taxes. As a result, a tax lien was entered against your property.

- **Paid Profit and Loss** — you eventually paid an account that was severely overdue.

- **Profit and loss Write Off** — creditor had to write your credit account off because you refused to pay the debt.

- **Account Closed** — Grantor's Request - creditor closed your account because you did not fulfill your credit obligation.

- **Settled for less than full balance** — you spent more then you can afford to repay.

- **120 days late payment** — you are extremely delinquent in paying your bills and there is a good chance that you will default on your account

- **90 days late payment** — you are three months behind in your bills.

- **60 day late payment** — you did not pay your creditor on time for two consistent months.

- **30 day late payment** — you did not pay your bills within 30 days following the due date.

How long will my delinquent student loan stay on my credit report?

As with unpaid tax liens, unpaid student loans can remain on your credit report indefinitely. If you pay off the student loan, the derogatory mark could remain on your credit report for up to seven years, because the payoff would begin the 7-year clock.

Did You Know?

If you become delinquent on your child support payments, it will be recorded against you on your credit reports.

Who has access to my credit report?

According to the Fair Credit Reporting Act, anyone seeking access to your credit file must have a permissible purpose. Creditors or third-party debt collectors may receive credit reports if the information is being used in connection with a credit transaction involving the collection of an account of the consumer.

CREDIT BUREAUS WILL PROVIDE A CREDIT REPORT UNDER THE FOLLOWING CIRCUMSTANCES ONLY

- As permitted by order of a court or federal grand jury subpoena per written permission from the consumer.
- For extension of credit as a result of an application from the consumer, or the review or collection of a consumer's account. *(ex. credit card companies, cell phone service providers, etc.)*
- For requesters who intend to use the information for employment purposes including hiring and promotion decision, where the consumer has provided permission.
- For the underwriting of insurance as a result of an application from the consumer.

Continued on page 50

Continued from page 49

- To determine a consumer's eligibility for a license or other benefit granted by a governmental instrumentality required by law to consider an applicant's financial responsibility or status.

- For the creditors who wish to review the consumer's account to determine if the consumer still meets the terms of their account.(ex. credit card companies).

- When there is a legitimate business need, as a result of a business transaction that is initiated by the consumer.

- For any purpose, if the consumer provides written permission.

Did You Know?

That there are two types of primary credit reports:

- **CONSUMER REPORT — the most common type of credit report. It is based on factual (but not always accurate) information about your bill-paying habits (whether you pay your accounts on time or late and if late, how late) and any public record information related to your finances: whether any of your creditors have "charged-off" a debt, whether you've filed for bankruptcy, or have a lien, court judgments, or other public record against you.**

- **INVESTIGATIVE REPORT — is a credit report that is based on interviews with employers, co-workers, neighbors or others and is most commonly used for employment or insurance investigations.**

When is my credit report free?

You are eligible to receive a free copy of your credit report if:

- **You have recently been denied credit or employment based on your credit report.** You have up to 60 days to request your free report and it must be from the same bureau that your creditor used to obtained your report.

- **You have recently been denied insurance based on your credit.**

- **You write a letter certifying that you are unemployed** and intend to apply for employment within 60 days.

- **You suspect that you are a victim of credit card/credit account fraud.**

- **You receive public welfare assistance.**

- **You live in Colorado, Georgia, Maryland, Massachusetts, New Jersey or Vermont** — You are eligible for a free copy of your credit report each year.

- **Due to a new law (see page 77) by September 2005 every United States citizen will have the right to receive a FREE credit report** annually from all 3 of the major credit bureaus.

What is the likelihood that I will find an error on my credit report?

It is highly likely that you may discover errors on your credit report. In 1998, The U.S. Public Interest Research Group conducted a study to examine the number and kinds of mistakes that could be found on a consumer credit report. Based on findings from the study "Mistakes Can Happen," an alarming number, approximately one-third of all consumer credit reports contain major errors that could cause unfair denial of credit for a car loan, mortgage, insurance or even a job.

According to the study:

- **Twenty-nine percent (29%)** of the credit reports pulled for the study contained serious errors including false delinquencies or accounts that did not belong to the consumer

- **Forty-one percent (41%)** of the credit reports contained incorrect personal demographic information such as the wrong or misspelled name, or long-outdated information, or addresses not belonging to the consumer.

- **Twenty percent (20%)** of the credit reports were missing well-established credit lines, such as loans, mortgages, or other consumer accounts critical to demonstrating the creditworthiness of the consumer.

- **Twenty-six percent (26%)** of the credit reports contained credit accounts that had been closed by the consumer but incorrectly remained listed as open.

Altogether, 70% of the credit reports contained either serious errors or other mistakes of some kind.

Examples of some of these errors include:

- **On-time payments being reported as late.**

- **Accurate information missing** because your creditor does not report to a credit bureau.

- **Information about someone else is included in your credit file** — it's usually someone with bad credit.

- **Accurate account reported twice** — making it appear that you are carrying too much debt/credit.

What happens to my credit report when I get married?

When you marry, your credit report stays the same. Only joint accounts or those for which one spouse is an authorized user show up on both credit reports. Since the credit bureaus only maintain files on individuals, your credit report is not impacted when you marry.

As with most credit accounts in which there is a joint account or you are an authorized user on someone else's account, the account history appears on both user's credit reports.

Joint credit card accounts are the responsibility of both individuals, even if one ran up the charges. To be released from the joint credit card debt, you must make arrangements with the creditor.

Here are some ways to manage your credit when you get married.

- Alert your creditors and the credit bureaus that you have changed your name, to ensure you don't lose your credit history.

- Keep and maintain some credit in your own name.

What Are Your Credit Accounts Saying About You?

(To ensure the integrity of your credit file you must check the following information for accuracy for all of your credit accounts and lines of credit.)

- The name of the creditor who has provided you with a line of credit.
- The date the account was opened
- The account credit limit
- The date of the last activity on the account
- The highest balance ever held on the account
- Terms of the credit account
- Your minimum monthly payment
- The current balance on the account
- The current amount past due

CREDIT REPORT ERRORS
(MORE COMMON THAN YOU THINK)

The Attorney General of New York estimates that one in every three credit reports contains errors

The Charles Givens Organization conducted a study in which 90% of the credit reports viewed contained errors.

EQUIFAX
CREDIT REPORT GUIDE

An Equifax credit report is divided into five parts:

1. **Personal Identification Information** — name, address, date of birth, social security number, telephone number, employer, employment information.
2. **Public Record Information** — which includes public notices such as bankruptcies, tax liens, and judgments.
3. **Collection Agency Account Information** — credit accounts placed with a collection agency will appear in this section. The name of the collection agency, and its telephone number is listed as well as the original creditor, the amount of the debt, the date the account was assigned to the collection agency, the account number and the last date of account activity.
4. **Credit Account Information** — includes all of the pertinent information regarding each tradeline and line of credit. The name of the creditor, account number, party responsible for the account, date the account was opened, number of months the account has been reviewed, date of last account activity, credit limit or highest balance, payment terms (ex. the amount of monthly payments), current balance, status of account, date the last entry was reported and payment history, can all be found in this section.

Collection Reported 07/03; Assigned 08/02 to CBE Group (300) 000-0000
Client - Directv; Amount - $104; Paid; Balance - $0
Date of Last Activity 07/02; Individual Account; Account Number 09878765

Company	Account #	Whose Acct	Date Opened	Months Reviewed	Date of Last Activity	High Credit	Terms	Items as of Date Reported			Date Reported
								Balance	Past Due	Status	
Americredit Finance AUTO	41289*	J	05/01	25	07/03	$9324	227	$6475	30	I1	07/03

5. **Companies that Requested Your Credit File** — In this section is listed the companies that have requested your credit file over the past 2 years. Inquiries with a PRM, AM or AR notation do not appear on the credit report that your creditors pull.

> **Did You Know?**
> **Lenders are as interested in the personal information on your credit reports as they are in your credit history. Everything listed on your report should be considered *worth verifying.***

I prefer to pay cash, so why must I establish credit?

With little to no credit history, you are rated a credit risk, even if you pay your bills on time.

If you fail to establish a good credit file, you will:

- Pay high interest rates for mortgages and other loans.
- Pay higher insurance premiums.
- Experience difficulty obtaining credit accounts.
- Limit your ability to use other people's money to build personal wealth.

SAMPLE EQUIFAX CREDIT REPORT

Hard Luck Credit Bureau
CREDIT FILE ❶
Confirmation # 567890

Please address all future correspondence to:
Credit Bureau Information Systems
1234 Big Brother Way
The Big 4, WJ
Phone: 999-999-0000
M - F 9:00am to 6:00pm in your time zone.

Please have a copy of this file, which displays a confirmation number, when calling Consumer Services for assistance. As information is updated regularly, please call us within 60 day from the date of this credit file.

Personal Identification Information

July 30, 2003

Renee D Crenshaw ❷
1234 North 5th Street
Prosperous Way, KOG

Social Security #: 100-000-0000
Date of Birth: July 4, 1900
Telephone: (200) 222-0000

Previous Address(es):
505 Invoice Road, Pay Off, FL 00000
532 Billinb Circle, Get Free, NW 00000

Last Reported Employment: Faithful Worker, Just Another Job Corporation
Previous Employment(s): Faithful Hard Worker, Just A Job Corporation

Collection Agency Account Information

Collection Reported 07/03; Assigned 08/02 to CBE Group (300) 000-0000 ❸
Client - Directv; Amount - $104; Paid; Balance - $0
Date of Last Activity 07/02; Individual Account; Account Number 09878765432445567

Public Record Information

Lien Filed 02/99; Case or Other ID Number-1234567; Amount-$5200 ❹
Class-State; Released 09/99; Verified 01/02

Credit Account Information *(For your security, the last 4 digits of your account numbers have been replaced by*)* ❺

Company	Account #	Whose Acct	Date Opened	Months Reviewed	Date of Last Activity	High Credit	Terms	Items as of Date Reported			Date Reported
								Balance	Past Due	Status	
Accredited Home Le REAL ESTATE MORTGAGE CONVENTIONAL MORTGAGE	1005*	I	11/00	21	02/03	$14400	151	$12000	M1		04/03
Capital One CREDIT	12345678909*	J	11/97	66	07/03	$1272	10	$347	60	R2	07/03
Sears CHARGE	90900078909*	I	11/97	66	07/03	$4040	11	$893		R1	07/03

Companies that Requested your Credit File ❻

07/30/03 Equifax Update
06/30/03 PRM - The Captus Group, Inc
06/19/03 AR - Capital One
05/15/03 PRM - Providian Financial Corp
09/06/02 Credit Bureau Associates

07/30/03 Consumerinfo.com
06/28/03 ID - Fair Issac & Company FICO
05/20/03 PRM - Well Fargo Financial
03/18/03 Discover Financial Services
07/31/02 AR IRWIN - Home Equity Corp.

SAMPLE EQUIFAX CREDIT REPORT KEY

1. **Credit Bureau Identifying Information** — Name and Address of the Credit Bureau that provided the report. If you plan to make your disputes via US Mail, this is the address you should be using.
2. **Personal Identification Information** — Which includes, your name, social security number, address, prior address, prior employer, current employer, telephone number, birthday and other identifying information.
3. **Collection Agency Account Information** — List of accounts your creditor has turned over to collection agencies.
4. **Public Record Information** — Information obtained from local, state and federal courts.
5. **Credit History Information** — Contains account information for both open and closed credit accounts.
   - a. **Company Name** — Identifies the company that is reporting the information.
   - b. **Account Number** — The account number for the account that is being reported.
   - c. **Whose Acct** — Indicates who is responsible for the account and the type of participation you have with the account.

"WHOSE ACCOUNT" CODES

J - Joint Account	**I - Individual**
A - Authorized User	**T - Terminated**
C - Co-Signer/Maker	**S - Shared**
B - On behalf of another	**U - Undesignated**
M - Maker	

d. **Date Opened** — Represents the month and year you opened the account with the creditor.

e. **Months Reviewed** — Number of months account payment history has been reported.

f. **Date of Last Activity** — This is the date of the last activity on the account which may include a payment, delinquency or change in the account.

e. **High Credit** — The highest amount charged or the credit limit.

g. **Terms** — Represents amount of monthly payment per month.

h. **Balance** — The amount owed on the account the date it is reported.

i. **Past Due** — Indicates any amount past due at the time the credit information is reported.

j. **Status** — Indicates the type of account and the timeliness of payments.

k. **Date Reported** — The last date the account information was updated.

EQUIFAX ACCOUNT "STATUS" CODES

Type of Account
Open - Entire Balance due each month *(ex. American Express)*
Revolving - payment amount variable (*ex. Credit Cards)*
Installment - fixed number of monthly payments *(ex. Auto Loan)*
Timeliness of Payments
0 - Approved not used; too new to rate
1 - Paid as agreed
2 - 30+ days past due
3 - 60+ days past due
4 - 90+ days past due
5 - Pays or paid 120+ days past due or collection account
7 - Making regular payments under a payment arrangement
8 - Repossession
9 - Charge off to bad debt

6 **Companies That Requested Your Credit File** - List of businesses that have received your credit report over the past 24 months. These requests are commonly know as inquiries.

INQUIRIES NOT REPORTED TO BUSINESSES

The following credit report inquiries do not show on your credit report when a business pulls your credit file. They only appear on copies of the credit report that is provided to you so that you may see who has had access to your credit information.

PRM — remain on your credit report for 12 months. This type of inquiry means that creditors are only provided your name and address, so that they may send you promotional credit offers.

AR/AM — remain on your credit report for 12 months. These inquiries indicate a periodic review of your credit account by your creditor.

Credit Bureau Inquiries — these inquiries are a result of activity by the credit bureau in response to your request for a copy of your credit

EXPERIAN
CREDIT REPORT GUIDE

The Experian Credit report is the most consumer friendly of all of the 3 major credit bureau's reports. The layout is simple and easy to understand. There are no codes or lettering system for consumers to try to decipher.

The credit report is divided into the following four parts:

1. **Potentially Negative Items** — this section includes all accounts that contain derogatory information, including late payments, delinquent child support, and collection accounts.

2. **Accounts in Good Standing** — includes all accounts without negative information. Listed in this section is the name of the creditor, the account number, account status, type of account, terms, credit limit, high balance, recent balance and payment, account history and balance history.

3. **Request for your Credit History** — contains a list of all those who have requested to review your credit history. The report lists the name of the creditor requesting your credit file, date of the request for your credit report, and the date when inquiry will be removed from your file. Also included in this section are the companies that requested your report but are not reported on the credit report that your creditors receive. These inquiries are from companies who are screening your account to see if you qualify for pre-approved credit offers. Also creditors with whom you currently have accounts will periodically pull your credit report to see if you still meet their credit criteria. If you do not, you could experience a interest rate increase.

4. **Personal Information** — includes name, address, social security number, year of birth, employers, telephone numbers, address, and type of residence.

SAMPLE EXPERIAN CREDIT REPORT

Report Number
0909090909090

Online Personal Credit Report from Experian for
Renee Denise Crenshaw

Report Date: June 16, 2001

Index:

- Potentially Negative Items
- Accounts in Good Standing
- Requests for Your Credit History
- Personal Information

Credit Bureau consumer information and disclaimer.

Potentially Negative Items

Credit Items

For your protection, the last few digits of your account numbers do not display.

SEARS

Address:
13200 Reality RD
Cleveland, OH 44130

Account Number:
375850900...

Status:
Open/Current, was past due 30 days

Status Details:
As of 11-2002, this account is scheduled to go to a positive status.

Date Opened: 08/1985	**Type:** Revolving	**Credit Limit/Original Amount:** $4,040
Reported Since 05/1994	**Terms:** NA	**High Balance:** $2,342
Date of Status: 12/1995	**Monthly Payment:** $0	**Recent Balance:** $0 as of 06/2001
Last Reported: 06/2001	**Responsibility:** Individual	**Recent Payment:** $0

Account History:
30 days as of 11-1995

Balance History:
$0 05/2001
$101 04/2001
$75 02/200
Between 10-1999 and 5-2001, your credit limit/high balance was $4,040

Accounts in Good Standing

City Mortgage Services

Address:
56 Gateway Rd
Cross Lanes, WV 25313

Account Number:
0092042710...

Status:
Paid/Never Late

Date Opened: 04/2000	**Type:** Installment	**Credit Limit/Original Amount:** $31,600
Reported Since	**Terms:**	**High Balance:**

Continued on page 64

Continued from page 63

09/2000	30 years	NA
Date of Status:	**Monthly Payment:**	**Recent Balance:**
03/2001	$294	$31,462 as of 03/2001
Last Reported:	**Responsibility:**	**Recent Payment:**
03/2001	Individual	$294

Requests for Your Credit History

Credit Bureau consumer information and disclaimer.

Discover
Address:
P.O. Box 29017
Phoenix, AZ 85038
Comments:
Permissible purpose. This inquire is scheduled to continue on record until 12-2002.

Date of Request:
11/21/2000

Requests Viewed Only By You

Premier Bankcard Inc
Address:
900 W Delaware Street
Sioux Falls SD 57104

Date of Request:
05/08/2001

Personal Information

Credit Bureau consumer information and disclaimer.

Name:
Renee Denise Crenshaw
Renee Crenshaw
Renee J Crenshaw

Address:
1899 Wisdom Road
Philadelphia, PA 19144
Type of Residence: Single Family
Geographical Code: 0-463940-101-6160

Social Security Number Variations:
19506064928

Year of birth:
1961

Employers:
Breakthrough International
Just Above Broke Corporation

Telephone numbers:
215-447-6607
215-444-5500

TRANS UNION
CREDIT REPORT GUIDE

Similar to the Equifax credit report, the Trans Union credit report is divided into 5 sections. The sections are: Personal Identification Information, Public Record Information, Adverse Information, Non-adverse credit account information and Inquiries made by companies.

1. **Personal Identification Information** — includes your name, date of birth, social security number, current address, former address, last report employer, and date you were entered into the Trans Union database.

2. **Public Record Information** — includes bankruptcies, tax liens, judgments, and the status of each.

3. **Adverse Information** — includes any derogatory or negative information listed within your credit file. The negative information is displayed within brackets (><) near the upper portion of the credit report. Also listed is creditor and credit account information for each negative listing. The type of credit granted, designated user of the account, the most recent update, date the account was opened, the date the account was closed, the balance, past-due balance, payment terms, credit limit and highest amount owed.

4. **Non Adverse Information** — includes the same kind of information found in the adverse information section except there are no negative notations in this section. The accounts are all in good standing.

5. **Inquiries Made to Companies** — There are three parts to this section. The first part is seen by anyone who pulls your credit. The other two parts, however, are only seen by you.

The first part of this section lists all of the creditors who you have provided permission to pull your credit for the purpose of granting you credit, insurance, employment, etc.

Listed in the second part are creditors who are screening you to make you a preapproval offer for credit and the third part lists your present creditors who have pulled your credit report to review your most current credit status.

FINDING THE NEGATIVE STUFF ON YOUR CREDIT REPORT

Equifax:

- Any item preceded by ">>>>"
- Any item rated higher than M1, R1 or I1
- Any collection notation, either paid or unpaid
- Any item listed as: Possession, Foreclosure, Profit and Loss write off, settled for less than full balance, settled, Included in bankruptcy, charge-off, paid profit and loss write-off,
- Any court account, including divorce, liens, judgments, etc.
- Any item showing 30,60, or 90-day late payments
- Any inquiry

Experian:

- Any item with an asterisk (*)
- Any inquiry

Trans Union:

- Any item in the adverse section of the report.
- Any information marked by >brackets<
- Any inquiry

SAMPLE TRANS UNION CREDIT REPORT

Your Trans Union File Number:
1234567890

For your protection,the last few digits of your account numbers do not display.

Consumer Report For
Crenshaw, Renee, Denise
2835 North Prosperity Lane
Peace Place, KOG 19259

Social Security Number:100-00-0000
Birth Date: 07/1955
You Have Been In our Files Since: 08/1981
Phone: 215-222-2222

Former Addresses Reported:
800 N. Lookout Lane, Tension, NN 20220

Employment Data Reported:

Just Over Broke, Inc
Date Reported: 06/2001

Take This Job and Shove It, Corp
Position: Paid Help

Date Reported: 08/1999

Your Credit Information

The following accounts contain information which some creditors may consider to be adverse. Adverse account information may generally be reported for 7 years from the date of the first delinquency, depending on your state of residence. The adverse information in these accounts has been printed in >Brackets< for your convenience, to help you understand your report. They are not bracketed this way for creditors.

>Collection Record<
The CVV Group Inc - Former # 4567890 — Collection Account
>Paid Collection< — Collection Agency/Attorney
Individual Account

Updated	07/2003	Balance:	$0
Placed	08/2002	Most Owed:	$104
Paid Off	10/2002		

>Status As of 10/2002: Paid Collection<

The following accounts are reported with no adverse information]

MBNA America #45677998849494949494
Revolving Account
Credit Card
Individual Account

Updated	12/2003	Balance:	$4039
Opened	03/1994	Most Owed:	$7681

Pay Terms: Minimum $111
Credit Limit: $7600

Status as of 12/2003: Paid or paying as agreed
In Prior 48 months from last update never late

Wells Fargo #45677998849494949494 Installment Account
Note Loan
Individual Account

Updated	10/2003	Balance:	$950
Opened	05/2003	Most Owed:	$1368

Pay Terms: 36 Monthly $38

Status as of 10/2003: Paid or paying as agreed
In Prior 6 months from last update never late

Companies that request your credit report must first provide certain information about you. Within the past 90 days, companies that requested your report provided the following information.

Subscriber Name	Date
T-Mobile	12/30/2003
Identifying information they provided:	
Crenshaw, Denise	
2835 North Prosperity Lane	

The Companies listed below received your name, address and other limited information about you so they could make a firm offer of credit or insurance. They did not receive your full credit report, and these inquiries are not seen by anyone but you.

Subscriber Name	Date
First USA DBA Bank One	09/2003
Capital One Bank	08/2003
Chase Manhattan Mortgage	07/2003

The Companies listed below obtained information from your consumer file for the purpose of an account reviewed or other business transaction with you. These inquiries are not displayed to anyone but you and will not affect any creditor's decision or any score.

Subscriber Name	Date
Renee Crenshaw via True	12/2003
Permissible Purpose = Consumer Request	
Americredit	12/2002
Lord & Taylor	07/2002

TEACH THE CHILDREN

Parents, teach your children about credit and help them establish a good credit record early so that hopefully they won't make mistakes that will damage their credit status. Building credit at an early age and knowing what to do with it can open many doors of opportunity for financial independence and success.

Common credit bureau codes:

Depending on the bureau, you may see the following codes on your credit report.

Notations for revolving credit accounts (e.g. credit cards)

R1..........Stands for current

R2..........Stands for slightly delinquent, usually 30 days

R3..........Stands for 60 days delinquent

R4..........Stands for 90 days delinquent

R5..........Stands for 120 days delinquent

R6..........Stands for 180 days delinquent

R7..........Stands for over 180 days delinquent

R8, **R9** ...Stands for charge-off, collections, or repossession

C............Current

N............Current account/zero balance

0 ....Current account/zero balance

1 ....30 days past the due date

2 ....60 days past the due date

3 ....90 days past the due date

4 ....120 days past the due date

5 ....150 days past the due date

6 ....180 days past the due date

7 ....Making regular payments or paid under wage earner plan or similar arrangements

8 ....Derogatory, repossession, foreclosure

9 ....Derogatory, collection, charge off

- ....No history reported for that month

Payment History Descriptions:

By now, hopefully, it has become apparent that to be successful in taking control of your credit, you must be knowledgeable about your current credit standing and have a good grasp of what's on your credit report.

As you can see, there are many factors that you need to know to understand your report. Listed below is additional information that may be used to note payment history on your credit report.

Bk Adj Plan — Debit included in or completed through a Bankruptcy Chapter 13.

Bk Liq Reo — Debit included in or discharged through Bankruptcy Chapter 7 or 11.

Charge Off — Unpaid balance reported as a loss

Clos INAC — Closed inactive account.

Clos NPAA — Credit line closed and not paying as agreed.

Coll Acct — Account Seriously past due. Assigned to the creditors internal collection department or assigned to a collection agency/attorney.

CR CD Lost — Credit card lost or stolen.

CR Ln Clos — Credit line closed by consumer request.

CR Ln Rnst — Account now available for use; in good standing.

Curr Acct — Either an open or closed account in good standing.

Cur was Col — Current account was a collection account.

Cur was Dl — Current account was past due.

Cur was For — Current account. Foreclosure was started.

Cur was 30-2, or 3, 4, 5, 6+ — Current account was 30 days past due two, three, four, five, six or more times.

Cur was 60, or 90, 120, 150, 180 — Current account was 60 or 90, 120, 150, 180 days late on payment.

Deceased — Consumer is deceased.

Delinq 60, or 90, 120, 150, 180 — Account 60 or 90, 120, 150,180 days late.

Del was 90 — Account was delinquent 90 days/now 30 or 60 days late.

Gov Claim — Claim filed with government for insured portion or balance on an educational loan.

Foreclosure — Credit grantor sold collateral to settle a mortgage that is in default.

Inquiry — A copy of the credit report that is sent to the credit grantor that has just requested it.

Ins Claim — Claim filed for payment of insured portion of balance.

Judgment — Lawsuit that resulted in a judgment against you and not paid.

Lien — Either federal, state or county taxes owed.

Not Pd AA — Account not being paid as agreed.

Paid Acct — Closed account with a zero balance, not rated by grantor.

Paid Status — Closed account, paid satisfactorily.

Pd by Dler — Credit grantor paid by company that originally sold the merchandise.

Pd Chg off — Paid account. Was a charge off.

Pd Coll Acc — Paid account. Was a collection account.

Paid not AA — Paid account. Some of the payments were made past the agreed due dates.

Pd Repo — Paid account. Was a repossession.

Pd was 30 — Paid account. Was past due 30 days.

Pd was 30-2, or 3, 4, 5, 6+ — Paid account.
Was past due 30 days 2 times, or 3, 4, 5, 6 or more times.

Pd was 60, or 90, 120, 150, 180 — Paid account.
Was late 60 or 90, 120, 150, 180 days.

Redmd Repo — Account was a repossession, now is redeemed.

Refinanced — Account was refinanced.

Repo — Merchandise was taken back by the credit grantor.

SCNL — Credit grantor cannot locate the consumer.

Settled — Via a settlement account paid in full for less than full balance.

Volun Repo — Voluntary repossession.

30 Day Del — Account past due 30 days.

30-2, or 3, 4, 5, 6+ times — Account past due 30 days 2 or 3, 4, 5, 6 or more times.

30 was 60 — Account was delinquent 60 days. Now 30 days late.

Did You Know?

There are sharks out there waiting for you. When you have bad credit, predatory creditors are seeking you out because they know that when you have bad credit your opportunities to obtain credit are limited. Therefore, check out all credit offers thoroughly before signing on the dotted line so that you don't get taken advantage of by a unscrupulous creditor.

6 REASONS TO CHECK YOUR CREDIT REGULARLY

1. **Mistakes Can Happen**
   Inaccuracies on a credit report is not a rare occurrence. The inaccuracy could be a payment not credited to data mixed in from the credit file of someone else with a name similar to yours. Your credit file is a living document and changes regularly without your knowledge or approval. Credit Reports and Credit Scores are used to make important decisions about issues that concern your life and financial well being, such as - How much you will pay for credit in the form of interest rates, and How much you will pay for car insurance, etc. With so much riding on your credit it is imperative that you check your credit report regularly, so you may address inaccurate information in a timely and efficient manner.

2. **Verify Payments**
   You should ensure that your payments are being recorded accurately on your credit report. Anything can happen to cause your payment to be late or not be credited to your account (ex.payment lost in the mail or payment credited to another customer's account in error) by your creditors in a timely manner. When you are monitoring your credit on a regular basis, you can contact your creditor and get the information corrected quickly. Also, if it is your fault that your payment arrived late, some creditors remove the delinquency as a courtesy if you are normally a good, consistent paying customer. The sooner you caught the problem and bring it to your creditor's attention the better!

3. **Identity Theft**
   Identity theft occurs when someone assumes your name and social security number to open new accounts. The culprit will provide the potential creditor with another address and charge up all kinds of debt without your knowledge. Most people never learn of the theft of their identity until their credit has been severely damaged and collectors are knocking at their door to recover the debt that was accumulated by the thief. If not addressed, the damage done by identity theft can jeopardize your ability to obtain credit in the future. The best way to catch a thief who is using your name is to get a copy of your credit report and ensure there are no new accounts that you have not opened or any other unusual activity.

4. **Too Many Credit Inquiries**
   Too many credit inquiries can make getting credit more difficult. Too many inquiries can actually lower your credit score and may cause a creditor to view you as a high credit risk. Therefore, it is important to keep inquiries to a minimum. It is not uncommon to find unauthorized credit inquiries on your credit report. If you didn't authorize someone to look at your credit report and they did, they may have broken the law, and you can request that the credit bureau remove these unauthorized inquiries from your credit file.

5. **Unauthorized Charges**
   This is a form of credit fraud that involves the theft of your credit card or account number to make unauthorized charges to your account. Although these may not be your charges, other creditors seeing the increased activity may decide to raise your interest rates. When you review your credit report on a regular basis you can catch new activity on accounts that you haven't been using or may have closed.

6. **Before Seeking Credit - Know Where You Stand**
   Thinking about buying a home or a new car? You need to know your credit score and what's in your credit report before seeking credit so that you can have a good idea of what you can expect to pay for the credit you seek. Also, knowing your creditworthiness can protect you from being victimized by predatory lenders.

Did You Know?

Although by law you can not be denied credit solely based on your age, a creditor may consider age as it relates to particular aspects of your creditworthiness. For example, if you are 69 and apply for a 30-year mortgage, a lender may be concerned that you may not live long enough to repay the loan. However, if you apply for a shorter loan term and increase your down payment, you might stand a better change of getting financed.

Why should I get my credit report and score?

Having your credit report and score will provide you with an idea of how a prospective creditor will see you. You need to have an idea of your total credit picture before applying for credit so that you know where you stand.

How do I order my credit report and score?

You may order both your credit report and score directly from the three major credit bureaus. You may order your report and score, via telephone, by mail or online. If you order online you will get your report immediately and you may download the information, review it and even dispute inaccurate information onlne. If you call or request via mail it may take 5 to 10 business days to receive your report, and you may dispute via telephone and in writing upon reviewing your report. Please note, you must have the file number or confirmation number provided on the report to dispute items on your credit report. The average cost for both the credit report and score is $12.95.

Did You Know?

Not having at least one credit card lowers your credit score. Not using the credit you have also lowers your credit score. If you never use credit, lenders can not assess your creditworthiness.

Get Your Credit Reports from the Nationwide Credit Bureaus for Free

Because of a new federal law, the Fair and Accurate Credit Transaction Act, better know as FACT, you now have the right to get a free copy of your credit report once every 12 months from each of the major credit reporting bureau - Experian, TransUnion and Equifax.

The act is being implemented in 4 phases with the first phase beginning December 2004 with the western states and shall continue until it is rolled out to all of the United States including US territories and possessions by no later than September 2005.

Phase 1

Effective December 1, consumers living in the western states listed below will have the right to order a free copy of their credit.

Alaska, Arizona, California, Colorado, Hawaii, Idaho, Montana, Nevada, New Mexico, Oregon, Utah, Washington, and Wyoming

Phase 2

Consumers in mid-western states will get this new right beginning March 2005.

Illinois, Indiana, Iowa, Kansas, Michigan, Minnesota, Missouri, Nebraska, North Dakota, Ohio, South Dakota and Wisconsin

Phase 3

Consumers in southern states will be eligible beginning June 2005.

Alabama, Arkansas, Florida, Georgia, Kentucky, Louisiana, Mississippi, Oklahoma, South Carolina, Tennessee and Texas

Phase 4

Consumers in eastern states, Puerto Rico and U.S. territories will be able to order reports starting September 2005.

Connecticut, Delaware, District of Columbia, Maine, Maryland, Massachusetts, New Hampshire, New Jersey, New York, North Carolina, Pennsylvania, Rhode Island, Vermont and Virginia,

Get Your Credit Reports from the Nationwide Credit Bureaus for Free

Want to avoid the trouble of contacting all 3 credit bureaus individually to get your FREE credit report? If you live in one of those states where the law has been implemented already, you can get your reports in one easy step.

As stated on the prior page, by September 2005 every United States citizen will have the right to order an annual FREE credit report from all 3 of the major credit bureaus. To make the process more user friendly a new process has been developed to make ordering your FREE credit reports from Trans Union, Experian, and Equifax a breeze.

With one single request via a central website, toll-free number or U.S. mail, you can order all three reports at once and won't have to bother with contacting each credit bureau individually.

For instant access to your FREE annual credit reports visit:

- **www.annualcreditreport.com**
- **or call 877-322-8228**
- **or download an Annual Credit Report Request Form at: www.ftc.gov/bcp/conline/edcams/credit/docs/fact_act_request_form.pdf.**

Complete the form, print it and mail to the address listed in the instructions.

For those living in those in states where the law is yet to be implemented, don't be discouraged, you can take advantage of this resource as soon as the FREE annual credit reports are available in your state.

Did You Know?

By law Credit Bureaus are not required to remove a Chapter 13 bankruptcy after seven years. The Fair Credit Reporting Act allows a credit bureau to report even a Chapter 13 bankruptcy for 10 years. Experian usually removes a Chapter 13 bankruptcy filing seven years after filing, so does TransUnion and Equifax. The seven-year time period is for discharged or dismissed Chapter 13 filings only.

CREDIT SCORING

A good credit score can change your life for the better by providing opportunities to access other people's money to invest into your dreams.

CREDIT SCORING

What is credit scoring?

Credit scoring is the use of statistical models to assess an individual's level of credit risk and credit worthiness based on the information contained in their credit file. Simply said, the score measures your ability to repay your loan. Credit scoring plays a major role in a creditor's decision to extend credit to you, and influences how much you will pay for that credit.

Credit scores, provided to creditors and consumers by credit bureaus, are calculated by a system of scorecards developed through the use of mathematical formulas and credit information for millions of people. These scorecards are designed to predict future credit risk and forecast repayment performance based on consumer credit management patterns.

The most widely used credit scoring system is FICO, developed by the Fair Isaac Corporation. The FICO scoring system produces a three-digit credit bureau score referred to as a FICO score. Equifax, Trans Union and Experian have their own version of the FICO scoring software that has been adapted to meet their specifications. Some creditors have their own customized scoring software as well.

What is FICO?

FICO is an acronym that stands for the Fair, Isaac and Company. FICO developed the credit score rating system and software used by the three major credit agencies (Equifax, Experian and Trans Union) and most lenders to calculate consumer credit scores.

How does FICO calculate my credit score?

Actually, FICO does not calculate your credit score, they develop and sell the credit scoring programs to credit bureaus. Equifax, Trans Union, and Experian have their own customized version of the FICO credit scoring software. Your FICO scores are calculated using a series of scorecards (designed for each bureau by FICO) that rate the information contained in your credit file. Each of the three credit bureaus have its own unique version of the FICO scorecards residing within its credit scoring software. The FICO score is called:

- Beacon at Equifax (there is believed to be 5 versions in use)
- Emperia at Trans Union (there is believed to be 2 versions in use)
- FICO at Experian (there is believed to be 2 versions in use)

Did You Know?

One way to quickly increase your credit score is to ask your creditor to remove a derogatory mark from your credit file. If you have a credit account such as a credit card, automobile loan, etc, where you have only one late payment, as a courtesy, per your request, the lender may remove it.

Let's face it, things happen; the cares of the world and everyday life sometimes causes us to forget to make a payment on time. If you have a good payment record, your creditor may be more than willing to remove a late mark from your credit file.

When approaching your lender, remain kind and courteous. Remember, you get more bees with honey than vinegar. Here is a script you may use when approaching your lender:

Hello my name is__________ I have an account with your company and have been a good customer. I am currently applying for a mortgage and noticed a late payment on my credit record. I don't recall ever being late, but am not denying that it might have happened by mistake or in error. Since I have been a solid paying customer, I was just wondering if you would as a courtesy remove the late payment from my credit file? Anything you can do would be greatly appreciated.

If the creditor agrees to remove the derogatory mark, make sure you get it in writing, and ask the creditor to report the change to the major reporting bureaus. Keep the letter in your file for proof that the creditor is removing the information. If the creditor does not report the change to the bureaus, you will have your copy of the letter that may be presented to the credit bureaus.

Common Mistakes that Can Lower your Credit Score

1. **Not Paying Your Bills within 29-days after the due date.**

   When you become past due by 30 or more days your creditor may report your account as delinquent to the credit bureaus. If you pay your bill within 29 days after the due date, your creditor cannot report you as late. Remember, you are not reported late until you are 30 or more days past your due date.

   For example: Your due date is September 1, you pay the bill September 29, your slow payment would not be reported to the credit bureaus.

2. **Not paying the minimum payment**

   Failing to pay the required minimum payment will result in your creditor reporting you as late to the credit bureau. If you are having difficulty paying the minimum, it is far better to contact your creditor and try to work out a payment arrangement.

3. **Maxing out credit cards**

   Maxing out your credit cards will affect your credit score substantially. Any account over 30% of the available credit limit will lower your credit score and may cause a lender to consider you a greater credit risk.

What is the range for credit scores?

Credit scores range between approximately 300 and 900. A score of 620 is the cutoff line for conforming (lower interest rate) loans. A score beneath 620 means more risk of default for the creditor.

WHAT'S YOUR CREDIT GRADE

Credit grades based on credit score

740 and Higher	**A+**
700 to 720	**A**
680 to 699	**A-**
660 to 679	**B+**
640 to 659	**B**
620 to 639	**C+**
600 to 619	**C**
599 and Below	**D-F**

Why is credit scoring used?

Credit scoring provide lenders with an objective and quick vehicle for evaluating your credit history and creditworthiness. If used correctly, credit scoring should enhance efficiency and consistency of the underwriting process.

What is a good credit score?

If your credit score is above 700, you are considered a good credit risk borrower and should have no problem getting a great interest rate on your home loan, car loan, or credit card. If your credit score is in the mid to upper 600's you are considered a "sub prime" borrower, and will likely pay a much higher interest rate on your loan. Below 560, you are going to have an extremely difficult time finding someone to finance your loan. The lower your credit score the more your insurance rates may be and the higher the interest rates you will pay to borrow money. With a score below 560, you still qualify for a credit card, but probably only a secured card and the interest rate will probably be very high — anywhere from 22 to 23%.

Why does the FICO score include inquiries?

The FICO scoring model considers inquiries because research has shown that those anticipating financial troubles try to increase the number of credit lines they have available.

Should I pay one credit card off or pay down all of them at once?

Pay down your cards, but do not close the accounts because that may negatively effect your debt to available credit ratio. Low balances mean a better credit score.

Work to get all your revolving credit (ex. credit cards, department store credit cards, lines of credit secured by real estate) at 30% or lower of your available credit balance. You may want to make a list of all of your credit cards with their available credit lines and determine what 30% of the total available credit is and try to maintain your revolving credit line balances at that number or lower. See the chart below for an example.

Your ultimate goal should be to completely pay down your credit cards.

CREDIT CARDS	AVAILABLE CREDIT	30% OF CREDIT LINE
Orchard Visa	$5,000	$1,500
Citibank MasterCard	$2,500	$750
Wachovia Visa	$1,000	$300

HOW CREDIT SCORES EFFECT A MORTGAGE APPLICATION

720 or above	A fairly quick and easy approval (1 to 2 weeks) because the risk for default is considered to be very low. Less emphasis will be placed on the debt to income ratios in determining the creditworthiness of the borrower. The lender may perform a quick overview of the credit file to ensure that all significant credit information is reflected in the credit score. Credit or inquiry explanations will not be required. Borrower will receive the prime interest rate.
660 to 719	The risk is considered reasonably low. The lender will in most cases check the credit file more closely for completeness. As a result, the approval may take a little longer (2 to 3 weeks) than for those with higher scores. In most instances, credit or inquiry explanations will not be required. Borrower will still receive good interest rates, but probably not as good as prime.
620 to 659	The risk of default is considered higher for the lender. To be approved for a mortgage loan, the lender will have to do a complete credit file assessment. Therefore it may take anywhere from 3 to 4 weeks to receive an approval if there are no multiple layers of risk present such as a high debt to income ratio. Borrower may still be eligible for decent interest rates, but will definitely pay much more for the same loan.
619 or below	The risk of default is considered extremely high and there is a possibility that the consumer will not find financing. However, the mortgage could be approved by a sub prime lender within 4 to 8 weeks, but the interest rates will be extremely high. The lender will go through the credit file thoroughly, and may require written explanations for derogatory information. Beware of predatory lenders who prey on those with poor credit.

What is the purpose of the FICO credit rating system?

The purpose of the FICO rating system is to provide the creditor with an idea of your creditworthiness and the level of risk you currently represent. The FICO system is a risk-based credit scoring tool that assigns your score based on a number of factors designed to assess your creditworthiness. In other words, the creditor is considering your creditworthiness based on the level of risk that the scoring instrument assigns to you through the vehicle of a credit score. The credit rating system is designed to give the creditor an indication of how likely it is that you will repay your loan, and provides the parameter for creditors to determine if they will extend you credit and at what cost.

Could auto insurance premium increase because of bad credit?

Several years ago, insurance companies began using credit scores to determine your level of risk before they sell or renew auto, home or renter policies. The insurance industry believes there is a direct correlation between financial stability and the potential that you will file a claim, and between bad credit and bad drivers.

Even if you have always paid your premiums on time and never filed an insurance claim you can still suffer the sting of bad credit that will result in unfavorable insurance rates. The use of credit scoring means your auto insurance premium will no longer be based on your driving record, but instead your credit score.

Many view the use of credit scores to determine eligibility for insurance as an unfair and discriminatory practice because insurance rates should be based on the merit of your actions not your credit score.

Did You Know?

Insurers that use credit scores as a determining factor for insurance eligibility and insurance premiums, could raise your rates or deny you insurance based on the following scenarios:

- You did not pay a credit card bill on time
- You have a large number of credit cards
- You have a large number of open credit accounts
- You switched credit cards to get a better interest rate
- You have a large outstanding balance on a credit card
- You take out a loan for any reason
- You pay the majority of your bills by cash or money order

All of the items listed above could lower your credit score.

Why was I told that I do not have a credit score?

Scoring is dependent upon sufficient and current information. The model can only score a file that has at least one account opened for at least six months and that satisfies both of the following conditions:

- A status date within the last six months, or if the status is not "current account" then a balance date within the last six months.
- Contains no disputed information. If a score cannot be calculated, an exclusion code will be supplied.

Did You Know?

You can hurt your credit rating if you do not carry a balance on your credit cards. When you do not use your credit cards there is no record of how you pay your bills. Without a record of how you pay your bills the FICO scoring system considers you a high credit risk.

WHAT'S NOT INCLUDED IN A FICO SCORE

The FICO Score does not consider the following factors when your credit score is calculated:

- Salary or other income.
- Race, Color, Religion, National Origin.
- Sex, Marital Status, Age.
- Occupation, Title.
- Employer, Employment History.
- Where You Live.
- Any interest rate being charged on a particular credit card or other account.
- Any items reported as child/family support obligations or rental agreements.
- Credit Counseling accounts.
- Certain types of inquiries (such as promotional, account review, insurance or employment-related inquiries).
- Any information not found in your credit report.

What are reason codes and how do they effect my credit score?

When the credit bureaus provide your lender with a FICO score, the score is accompanied by what are called "reason codes." The reason code tells which scorecard factors lowered your score.

It is used by lenders to provide you with an explanation for denying your request for credit. For you, the reason codes could be very important, since they will indicate the best ways to improve your score.

An example of some of the reasons your request for credit might be denied include the following score reason codes:

- Amount owed on accounts is too high;
- Delinquency on accounts;
- Too few bank revolving accounts;
- Too many bank or national revolving accounts;
- Too many accounts with balances;
- Consumer finance accounts;
- Account payment history is too new to rate;
- Too many inquiries in last 12 months;
- Too many accounts opened in last 12 months;
- Proportion of balances to credit limits is too high;
- Amount owed on revolving accounts is too high;
- Length of revolving credit history is too short;
- Time since delinquent is too recent or unknown;
- Length of credit history is too short;
- Lack of recent bank revolving account information;
- No recent non-mortgage balance information;

- Number of accounts with delinquency;
- Too few accounts currently paid as agreed;
- Time since derogatory public record or collection is too short;
- Amount past due on accounts;
- Serious delinquency, derogatory public record or collection;
- Too many bank or national revolving accounts with balances;
- No recent revolving balances;
- Proportion of loan balances to loan amounts is too high;
- Lack of recent installment loan information;
- Date of last inquiry too recent;
- Time since last account opening is too short;
- Number of revolving accounts;
- Number of bank revolving or revolving accounts;
- Number of established accounts;
- No recent bankcard balances;
- Too few accounts with recent payment information.

Did You Know:

The only credit bureau that provides consumers with the same FICO credit score that lenders receive is Equifax. The scores provided to consumers by Experian and Trans Union are not FICO scores, and are different from the credit scores provided to lenders.

What factors are used to determine my FICO credit score?

The 5 prominent factors that affect your FICO credit score are:

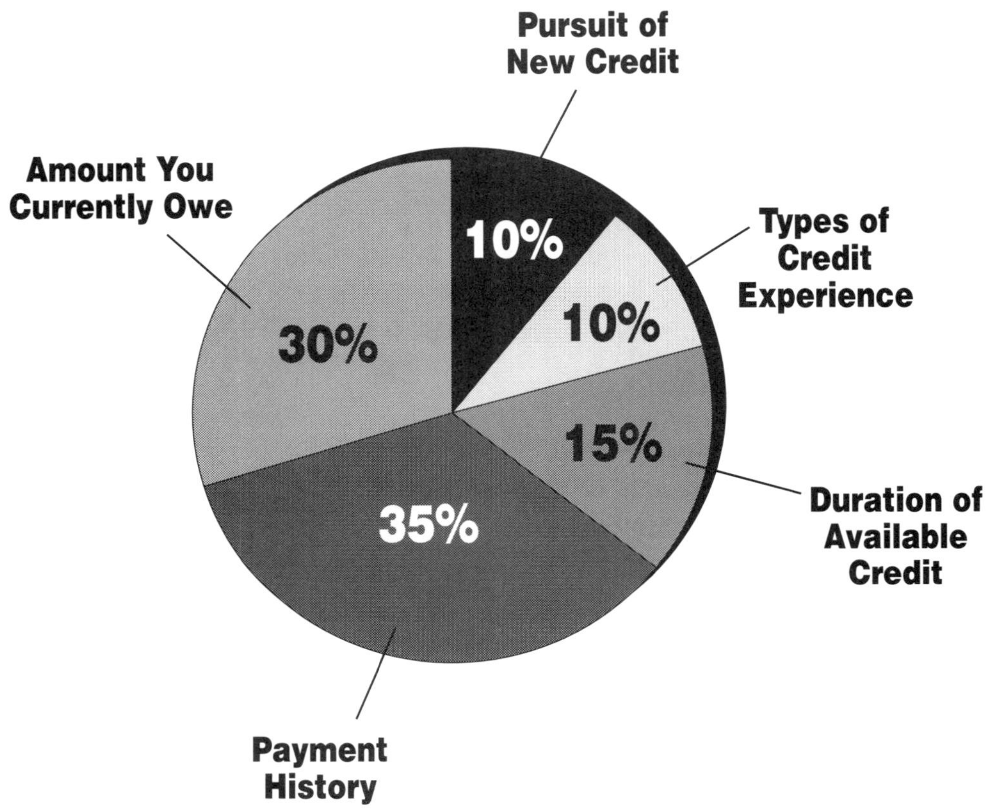

1. **Payment History - 35%**
   How is your payment history? Your lender wants to make sure that you are paying your bills. Although just one of the factors used in calculating your credit score, it is the one that carries the most weight. Your credit history includes all credit activity including credit cards, mortgages, lines

of credit, auto loans, collection items and public records, which could include judgments, liens, bankruptcies, suits, and wage garnishments. FICO considers if you pay your creditors on time, whether you have delinquencies, how recent and frequent.

The factors in this group include:

- Account payment information on specific types of accounts *(credit cards, retail accounts, installation loans, finance company accounts, mortgage, etc.)*
- Presence of adverse public records *(bankruptcy, judgments, suits, liens, wage attachments, etc.)* collection items, and/or delinquency *(past due items)*
- Severity of delinquency *(how long past due)*
- Amount past due on delinquent accounts or collection items
- Time since (recency of) past due items *(delinquency)*, adverse public records *(if any)*, or collection items *(if any)*
- Number of past due items on file
- Number of accounts paid as agreed

To improve your credit score in this factor, maintain a long-term good payment track record with your creditors.

2. **Amount you Currently Owe - 30%**

   The lender wants to know if you are carrying too much debt. Carrying too much credit is held against you even if you do not have balances on your credit cards. The lender wants to ensure that you can comfortably pay your debt with them and your other creditors.

   Your level of debt is determined by considering the amount of credit you are currently using and the amount of credit you still have available. The total balance and total credit limit across all credit trade lines is used to compute your FICO score.

Factors in this group include:

- Amount owing on accounts
- Amount owing on specific types of accounts
- Lack of a specific type of balance, in some cases
- Number of accounts with balances
- Proportion of credit lines used (proportion of balances to total credit limits on certain types of revolving accounts)
- Proportion of installment loan amounts still owing (proportion of balance to original loan amount on certain types of installment loans)

3. **Duration of available credit - 15%**
   The duration of available credit is the number of months your credit accounts have been on your credit report. If the account is in good standing, the longer the credit history, the better. The credit scoring system considers the age of your oldest account, the average age of all your accounts, how long it has been since you used certain accounts and the mix of older and new credit accounts.

   Factors included in this section include:

   - Time since accounts opened
   - Time since account activity
   - Time since accounts opened, by specific type of account

4. **Pursuit of New Credit - 10%**
   Every time someone runs a credit check on you, whether you are searching for a new credit account or just rate shopping, it creates an inquiry, which is viewed as a negative mark on your credit report. However, mortgage and automobile inquiries are supposed to be grouped

and counted as one inquiry if the inquiries are within 14 days of each other. This special grouping was designed to avoid penalizing you when shopping for a good mortgage or auto rate.

In addition, the credit scoring model will ignore all auto and mortgage related inquiries that occur within a 30-day period before calculating your score.

Also, FICO takes into consideration how may new accounts have been opened within the last year and the number of inquiries in the last six months. Inquiries are factored as if you are searching for credit. Too many of these inquiries look bad on your credit report and will negatively effect your credit score. It is believed that credit inquiries can lower your score quite substantially - 20 to 40 points or more. No one knows for sure, because the actual point value is not disclosed. There are some inquiries that are not factored into your score; among them are routine credit checks by your current lender and inquiries made by you into your own account.

Factors in this group include:

- Number of recent credit inquiries
- Number of recently opened accounts
- Proportion of accounts that are recently opened, by type of account
- Time since credit inquiry

5. **Types of Credit Experience - 10%**
The types of credit include installment loans (ex. automobile loan, unsecured personal loans) retail accounts including department store credit cards, and mortgages. Too many finance company installment loans (*ex. Household, Beneficial, Wells Fargo)* can lower this score factor.

Factors included in this group include:

- Number of various types of accounts *(ex. credit cards, retail accounts, installment loans, mortgages, consumer finance accounts, etc.)*

I BET YOU DIDN'T KNOW...

Your credit card company pulls your credit reports regularly, to look for delinquencies, so that they may increase your interest rate. Even if you are a good customer and never missed a credit card payment, your credit card company will increase your interest rate if you have any late payments with one of your other creditors. If the credit card company discovers a delinquency, regardless of whether true or false, you are going to get an interest rate increase, or if your credit score drops below what would be considered acceptable, your interest rate may be raised anywhere from 5 to 10 percent.

Can credit inquiries damage my credit score?

Absolutely!! Multiple credit inquiries can take any where from 2 to 50+ points off of your credit score, the average is 3 to 35 points. Multiple credit inquiries in a short period of time is calculated by the credit scoring program as a negative factor. Research has shown that opening several credit accounts in a short period of time represents a credit risk.

There is no such thing as a good inquiry. Unfortunately, there is no specific value for inquiries. However, Fair Isaac estimates that multiple inquiries contribute less than 10% of the weight of your credit score.

Although there is no such thing as a good inquiry, the following inquiries will not damage your credit score:

- **Consumer Initiated** — inquiries made by the consumer through a credit bureau are not calculated in your score
- **Pre-approval Offers** — inquiries for the purpose of marketing by a bank or for credit solicitations. A potential creditor may send you a pre-approval offer but it is not counted as an inquiry against you until you accept the credit offer. Upon receipt of the offer, a full credit report will be pulled and the inquiry will be calculated against your credit score.
- **Periodic Review** — inquiries for the purpose of managing existing accounts. Many lenders review your credit report to see if you still meet their credit criterion. If you no longer do, the credit card company may increase your interest rate.

Because the system is designed to take into account rate shopping for automobiles and mortgages, multiple inquiries by automotive dealers and mortgage companies made within a 14 day period of time are counted as 1 inquiry. In addition, mortgage and auto inquiries will not be placed on your credit report until they are at least 30 days old. For example, if you are shopping for a mortgage and expect to purchase your new home within 30 days, the inquiry will not show up on your credit report for another 30 days. As a result the inquiry will not effect your credit score in those 30 days prior to purchasing your home.

TYPE OF CREDIT	# OF DAYS AGO	# OF INQUIRIES	COMMENTS
Department Store	67	1	Applied for 1 department store card
Mortgage Mortgage	65 56	1	Two mortgage applications within 14 days of each other counts as only 1 inquiry
Auto	15	1	Will be placed on credit report after 30 days.
Auto Auto	8 7	Not counted at all if within 14 days of the first auto inquiry	These two don't count at all as they were within 14 days of the first auto app
Bankcard	2	1	Applied for 1 credit card

How much will it cost me to borrow if I have low credit scores?

Unfortunately, you might be paying thousands of extra dollars in interest due to poor credit and as a result a higher payment for the same automobile and house as someone with stronger credit. I've provided you two examples of how interest rates are much lower for those with good credit.

Sample Automobile Financing — The table listed below gives you an idea of what your payments would be based on the condition of your credit.

$23,000 CAR PAID OVER 5 YEARS

CREDIT SCORE	RATE	PAYMENT	INTEREST PAID	TOTAL PAYMENT
Good	5%	$434.00	$3,042	$26,042
Fair	12%	$512.00	$7,697	$30,697
Poor	22%	$635.00	$15,114	$38,114

Sample Mortgage Financing — As displayed in the automobile financing example, the cost for having poor credit is great. In the example below, the new homeowner has made a $7,500 down payment on a $150,000 home.

$142,500 MORTGAGE PAID OVER 30 YEARS

CREDIT SCORE	RATE	PAYMENT	INTEREST PAID	TOTAL PAYMENT
Good	5%	$765.00	$125,400	$275,400
Fair	7%	$948.00	$191,280	$341,280
Poor	9%	$1,147.00	$270,420	$412,920

As you can see, when you have bad credit, you pay more for the privilege of credit. In the example above, you have the same house, same down payment, but the monthly mortgage payments are substantially different as well as the total cost of the house with principle and interest payments.

Why does my lender use a different credit score than the one I have?

Mortgage lenders review loan applications primarily in relation to risk. They make decisions based on many factors, not just credit scores. Lenders often consider income, how long you have lived at your current address, what kinds of assets you have, the balances in your checking and savings accounts, your promptness in paying bills, how long you have been working for the same company, and how much you owe other lenders to determine your level of creditworthiness and potential risk.

A mortgage credit score can be different by as much as 50 points than the online credit scores that consumers can purchase directly from the credit bureaus. While, the credit report information is the same, the score will be different due to customized filters that the lender has requested. Also, in addition to the customized FICO score that lenders use to evaluate your credit, some lenders also use their own in-house FICO credit scoring software.

Did You Know:

If you have bad to fair credit you should begin working on your credit at least 2 years in advance of applying for your mortgage.

Before applying for your next loan, check out the chart below to get an idea of how mortgage companies evaluate your creditworthiness. Here are examples of some of the numbers that mortgage lenders use to calculate your credit score, when using their in-house FICO credit scoring software.

CONSUMER TRAIT	CONSUMER STATUS	POINTS +/
OWN/RENT:		
	Own	25
	Rent	15
	Other	10
	No Information	17
YEARS AT CURRENT ADDRESS		
	<.5	12
	.5-2.49 Years	10
	2.5-6.49 Years	15
	6.5-10.49 Years	19
	>10.49 Years	23
	No Information	13
OCCUPATION:		
	Professional	50
	Semi Professional	44
	Manager	31
	Office Worker	28
	Blue Collar	25
	Other	22
	No Information	27

CONSUMER TRAIT	CONSUMER STATUS	POINTS +/
YEARS AT JOB:		
	<5 Years	2
	.5-1.49 Years	8
	1.5-2.49 Years	19
	2.5-5.49 Years	25
	5.5-12.49 Years	30
	>12.5 Years	39
	Retired	43
	No Information	20
DEPARTMENT STORE/ MAJOR CREDIT CARDS:		
	None	0
	Department Store	11
	Major Credit Card	16
	Both	27
	No Answer	10
	No Information	12
BANK REFERENCE:		
	Checking	5
	Savings	10
	Both	20
	Other	11
	No Information	9

CONSUMER TRAIT	CONSUMER STATUS	POINTS +/
DEBT RATIO:	<15%	22
	15-25%	15
	26-35%	12
	36-49%	5
	>50%	0
	No Information	13
NUMBER OF INQUIRIES:	0	3
	1	11
	2	3
	3-4	-7
	5-9	-20
	No Record	0
NUMBER OF REVOLVING LINES OF CREDIT:		
	0	5
	1-2	12
	3-5	8
	>6	-4
PERCENTAGE OF BALANCES AVAILABLE:		
	0-15%	15
	16-30%	5
	31-40%	-3
	41-50%	-10
	>50%	-18
DEROGATORY CREDIT:		
	No Record	0
	Any Derogatory Credit	-29

CREDIT
RESTORATION

Restoring your credit is a realistic and honorable goal and should be viewed as a business transaction.

CREDIT RESTORATION

Why would Credit Bureaus not want me to clean up my credit?

Credit bureaus are not in business to serve you. Every time credit information is challenged, the credit bureau is losing money. They make no money from investigating consumer disputes, but must do so by law.

Credit Bureaus are in business to provide their clients, lenders and creditors, with information about you, so that a lender may access their level of risk when they consider granting you credit. Therefore, it is to the credit bureau's advantage if you do not restore your credit, because it is better to have you evaluated as a greater credit risk regardless of whether it is true or not, than to report you below your actual risk level.

If it were easy to restore your credit, everyone would be doing it and those who consistently pay their bills late or do not pay their obligations at all would have as much creditworthiness as someone who does pay their bills on time. Also, the credit bureaus would go out of business because lenders would not have confidence in the credit information that the bureaus are supplying. It is believed that the entire credit report dispute process is designed to discourage you from restoring your credit.

Should I use a credit repair company to fix my credit?

While you have the right to ensure that your current credit information is accurate, it is a time consuming process that will take much patience and perseverance. I would suggest that you do it for yourself. Through the process you will learn a lot about your financial situation and how the credit system works. It is also an opportunity to learn how to manage your credit.

If you know that you do not possess the wherewithal to do the work or spend the time to restore your credit, you may want to consider a credit repair company.

However, I would advise you to beware of companies that:

- **Advise you to take any action that seems illegal.** *(e.g. creating a new credit identity)*
- **Advise you to use an Employer Identification Number** in place of your social security number.
- **Do not inform you of your legal rights** and what you can do yourself for free.
- **Require you to pay for credit repair services** before any services are rendered.

Are there any consumer laws in place for credit repair services?

Yes, the Credit Repair Organization Act was developed to protect consumers from unfair practices by credit repair companies.

The act requires credit report agencies to:

- Provide consumers with a copy of the "Consumer Credit File Rights" under state and federal law before you sign a contract for services.

- Provide consumers with a written contract that details the consumer's contractual rights and obligations.

A credit repair company cannot:

- Make false claims about their services.

- Charge you until they have rendered service.

- Perform any services on a consumer's behalf without their written signature on a contract.

- Perform any services until after three days from the time the contract was signed by the consumer. During the three-day waiting period the consumer may cancel the contract without penalty.

The contract must include:

- Company name and address.
- The total cost for services.
- The payment terms.
- A detailed description of the service being rendered.
- The time frame in which the results will be achieved.
- Any service guarantees offered.

Did You Know?

Under the Credit Repair Organizations Act,

credit repair companies cannot require you to pay

prior to the delivery of agreed upon services.

LOW REVOLVING CREDIT BALANCES = BETTER CREDIT SCORES

What happens when I dispute items on my credit report?

When you dispute an item on your credit report, the credit bureau is required to verify that the listing is correct for it to remain on your credit report. The information submitted by your creditor is presumed correct unless proven incorrect by you. If the creditor reports that the information is correct, and you know it to be incorrect, it is now your responsibility to inform the credit bureau that the information that the creditor has provided is inaccurate.

If the credit listing contains some inaccuracies, the credit bureau may simply change the item to correct the inaccuracies. Items that cannot be verified must come off of your credit report.

In some cases, the creditor either no longer possess the information or does not wish to go through the trouble of verifying it. The reinvestigation must be completed within 30 days or, by law, the listing must be removed.

Will paying off my outstanding bills repair my credit?

When it comes to credit scoring, paid off negative listings are no better than unpaid negative listings. Paying off the outstanding account will not add points to your credit score or remove the negative information from your credit report. Although creditors who are evaluating your credit may require that you pay any outstanding debt before they will grant you credit.

If you decide to pay off outstanding debt, you may want to consider:

- Negotiating with the creditor or the collection agency for an agreement to compromise debt and to remove the derogatory remark from your credit report in exchange for paying off the account. If you pay off the account without a signed agreement, and the creditor or collection agency does not remove the derogatory mark from your credit report, you will no longer have any leverage to negotiate. Therefore, make sure you get everything in writing before making the final payment. (see sample agreement to compromise debt on page 135)

- Pay off the outstanding account as quickly as possible, especially if the collection listing is fairly current, between 3 to 6 months old.

If I pay off old collection accounts will it affect the 7-year clock?

There has been some debate regarding this issue. Some believe that if you pay off a charge off or collection account it is not counted against you by the credit scoring program. Others believe that when you pay off the debt it is noted in the credit file under "Date of Last Activity" which is the date that FICO scoring models use to calculate your credit score and the starting point for the 7-year clock to begin.

A collection account was placed on my credit report on 07/2002, and I paid off the account on 10/2003. The "Date of Last Activity" did not change. Since there was no change, my paying the account off had no effect on my credit score, or the date that the collection would fall off of the credit report.

Paying off your debt is always the right thing to do and should be one of your highest goals. However wisdom should be used so that paying your debts won't backfire on you.

If you are planning to purchase a home, it is suggested you begin paying off your outstanding debt at least 2 years before you actually apply for your mortgage. However, if you are already in the process of applying for a mortgage, seek advise from your lender first before paying off any collection accounts.

Also, if you have collection/charge off accounts in your credit file, your mortgage lender may require you to payoff those accounts before they will approve your mortgage. However, you can ask the lender if you may pay off the existing charge off/collection accounts in escrow.

THE DO'S AND DON'TS DURING THE MORTGAGE PROCESS

- Do pay your bills. Even one late payment can negatively effect your credit score.

- Don't make any large deposits into your bank account without first speaking to your loan officer.

- Don't max out your credit cards. Maxing out your credit cards will devastate your credit score. Try to keep balances at or under 30% below your credit card limit.

- Don't let anyone use your credit or co-sign for anyone.

- Don't have anyone run your credit report because the inquiry will have a negative impact on your credit score.

- Don't buy a car or any other major purchases during the mortgage process.

- Don't change jobs. Lenders are looking for stability. Employment with a current employer of less than 2 years represents greater risk and may be rated as a negative factor.

How can I quickly improve my credit score?

One of the quickest ways to improve your credit score is to have your credit file rescored. Unfortunately, rescoring services are only offered to mortgage brokers and mortgage lenders. If you discover that there is an error on your credit report that is effecting your credit score and you need to have it rescored immediately so that you can qualify for the mortgage for your new home, your mortgage lender can contact a rescoring company that will investigate disputed items on your credit report and have your credit file updated in a matter of a few business days. Normally, it could take anywhere from 30 to 90 days for the credit bureaus to update your credit file.

With the proper documentation *(e.g., letter from the creditor, on the creditor's letterhead,* – verifying the mistake, copies of lien releases, paid receipts, etc.), the corrected information is sent to the credit bureaus by the credit rescoring company. The bureau will then investigate the dispute and correct the error.

Within 2 to 3 days your lender or mortgage broker can pull your new credit report and new credit scores. When significant errors are removed scores have been increased on an average of 50 to 100 points. The service cost anywhere from $75.00 to $250.

Boost Your Credit Score in 30 days or less

You can boost your credit score quickly by:

- Paying down all of your revolving credit accounts (e.g. credit cards, charge cards, lines of credit) to 30% of the available credit limit. After you have paid down the debt, call your creditor and ask them to update your credit file with the credit bureau. You may also dispute the current balances with the credit bureaus.

- Contact creditors that have placed derogatory information in your credit file and if you have been a good payer over the last 12 to 24 months, ask if they would remove the delinquency as a courtesy. Some creditors, such as Sears call these goodwill adjustments. Your chances of getting a goodwill adjustment become greater the longer the delinquency has been on your report. Also, if you have been an overall good payer but was late just once, the creditor is more inclined to remove the mark from your credit record. The quickest way to seek goodwill consideration is to contact the creditor by telephone. I have also included a Goodwill Letter for your use on page 132.

- If you have an unpaid collection account, contact the collection company and ask if they delete, meaning will they remove the debt from your credit report if you pay the debt off. In exchange for your paying the account in full, some collection agencies will report your collection account as "paid as agreed" instead of the negative notation of "collection paid or paid charge off." Make sure you get it in writing before paying off the debt, because if you pay off the debt first you will lose your power to negotiate.

Is it illegal to dispute items on my credit report?

No, according to the Fair Credit Reporting Act (FCRA), it is your right to dispute items on your credit report that are inaccurate. You should not lie or attempt to get over on the system, but you have every right to question anything and everything in your credit file, especially if you believe the information listed in your credit report is incomplete, inaccurate, or obsolete. When done properly, the credit repair is nothing more than exercising your rights under the FCRA.

How long will it take to repair my own credit?

If you are committed and organized it could take a year of diligent work. It really depends on the status of your credit when you begin this process.

When must bureaus remove derogatory information?

If a credit bureau cannot verify that the item you are disputing is indeed correct, it must remove the listing from its file regardless of whether the information is true or not.

How do I dispute incorrect information on my credit report?

The process for disputing incorrect information on your credit report is fairly simple and can be accomplished in a 4 step process.

1. Order your credit report and credit score either in writing, online or over the telephone. It is better to get your report online because you may also submit a dispute electronically via a user-friendly short form.

2. Upon receipt of your credit report, examine it for inaccurate, obsolete and/or incomplete information.

3. If you find any information that is inaccurate, obsolete or incomplete you have the right, by law, to dispute the inaccuracy with the collection bureaus.

4. Dispute the item(s) with the credit bureau(s) either by telephone, online or in writing. The credit bureau has 30 days to conduct their investigation and get back to you with their findings and the outcome. If the investigation is not completed within 30 days, the listing must be removed.

Note: older items may be more difficult to verify because the creditor may no longer have the records available to verify the information one way or another. Therefore, the information by law must be removed if it cannot be verified.

How can I stop collection agencies from bugging me?

The Fair Debt Collection Practices Act gives you the right to stop collection agencies from ever writing or calling you again. By law, a collection agency must cease and desist after you send them a letter instructing them to do so. If the collection agency fails to comply with the law, you have the right to take civil action against them. Make sure you send your letter via certified mail *(See Cease and Desist sample letter on page 128)*

GOOD RECORD KEEPING

When working to restore your credit it is important to keep good records. Make folders for each step of the process. You should have a folder for your credit report and score, your dispute letters, letters from creditors and the bureaus. Keep this information on file just in case you need to challenge any adverse information or action.

Did You Know?

You must have a credit report confirmation number or file number if you want to dispute items on your credit report. The only way to get a confirmation or file number is to buy a credit report or you may get one for free, if you meet certain requirements. (see credit report chapter) Credit bureaus will not serve you without a number.

How will I know if following a bureau investigation the inaccurate information was removed from my credit report?

Upon the conclusion of the credit bureau's investigation, a new copy of your credit report will be sent to you. This report is different than a normal report because it provides the results of the bureau investigation. The results of the investigation can be found in the front of the report. The report will tell you if the creditor verified the listing or if the item was deleted.

Can I create another credit file by using an EIN number?

This is an illegal scheme that could land you in jail. In essense, by using a Employer Identification Number, you will be using the number under false pretences on a loan application, which is a federal crime. It is also a federal crime to use an EIN as your social security number. If caught you could be charged with wire and mail fraud if you used the telephone to apply for the credit.

If by chance you have already done this, be thankful that you haven't been caught and don't do it again. If you are currently doing this, STOP immediately, because if you are caught, you are going straight to jail. Don't take a chance with your freedom.

Some Tips for Improving Your Credit

1. Don't miss any credit account payments.

Delinquent payments can devastate your score. One missed payment can reduce your credit score by 20 to 160 points.

SOLUTIONS:

Consider automating your bill payments. Through online banking services you can schedule bill payments so that they come out of your checking account at a scheduled time on a monthly basis.

Also, if you are getting close to the payment due date you may want to consider utilizing online or telephone bill-payment services.

- Online bill-payment services are offered by most banks, lenders and utility companies. For your convenience, many companies provide this service on their website for no additional charge. Please note that some lenders have a cut-off time for the day and will count your payment as being received on the following day if you do not meet that deadline. Therefore, it is important to know what the "end of business day" is for online payments so that you won't end up having your payment counted a day after you made the payment.

- Telephone payment services, such as Speedpay, are made available by some companies for clients who would like to make their payment via this automatic telephone system. The payment is usually considered received on the day you called it in. However, it may not actually be posted for 24 to 48 hours and there will be a fee anywhere from $1 to $15, depending on the lender/creditor.

2. Pay down all revolving credit.

It is better to have more credit cards with low balances than a few credit cards with balances that are close to the credit limit. It should be your goal to maintain a balance that is no more than 30% of your credit limit. If you can not pay down your credit balances immediately, consider requesting credit line increases to lower the credit balance/credit limit debt ratio. Any revolving credit account balance above 30% will negatively affect your credit score. Therefore, use caution when refinancing your home to consolidate your debt, especially if you are being granted a revolving line of credit. What some lenders fail to tell you is that although the line of credit is secured by your home, the loan is recorded on your credit report the same way a credit card is and as a result, if the balance you owe exceeds 30% of the credit limit you will damage your credit rating.

SOLUTION:

Pay down all of your credit cards to 30% of the credit card's credit limit as soon as possible. If you have lines of credit secured by property, you may want to consider applying for a "rate and term" mortgage. Through a "rate and term" mortgage you can pay off the line of credit, the new credit, and the line of credit would be replaced by the new mortgage. You will probably not receive any monies from this type of transaction, but could save money because the cost for a line of credit is more expensive than a mortgage and your credit score should improve drastically because the line of credit,which is revolving credit, will be paid off in full.

3. Don't be so quick to close old paid accounts

Closing accounts could hurt your credit score. Although having too many open accounts can damage your score, you will only actually make things worse from closing older accounts. Because the credit scoring software looks for credit history, shutting down older accounts can also make your credit history look younger than it actually is, which will hurt your overall score. The credit scoring software compares your total available credit limit to your total credit balance to determine credit risk. Shutting down credit accounts will lower your available credit and make your debt balance larger as a ratio, which will also hurt your credit.

SOLUTION:
Rotate and use all of your credit cards. An inactive credit card does not increase your credit score. Keep the balances on the active credit accounts below 30% of the available credit line. If you have credit cards with balances over 30%, you may want to transfer some of those balances over to the card with the $0 balances to increase your credit score. Lastly, If you feel that you really must get rid of credit cards, keep the ones that have the longest positive credit history and the highest credit limit.

4. Avoid applying for unnecessary credit

Applying for credit will generate credit inquiries on your credit report which has a negative effect on your credit report.

SOLUTION:
Limit your inquiries to no more than two to three per year and challenge any inquiry on your credit report that you do not recognize.

5. Check your credit on a regular basis

It is extremely important for you to take control of your credit. You need to know who is looking at your credit report and how your lenders/creditors are reporting your credit information. It has been proven over and over again that human error does occur at the credit bureau level. Therefore, you must add this step to your financial fitness plan to ensure your credit remains healthy.

SOLUTIONS:

Order your credit report and score from all three major credit agencies at least once a quarter. Review the information carefully and dispute any information that is inaccurate, incomplete or obsolete.

6. Validate credit accounts that have been assigned to collection agencies.

If a credit collection agency contacts you with the intent to collect on a debt, you have the right, within 30 days of receiving a written notice, to request that the collection agency validate the alleged debt. *(see sample Validation letter on page 133)*

7. Avoid having too many finance company loans

Having finance company loans on your credit report has a negative effect on your credit report and credit score because finance company loans are seen as loans designed for people who have bad credit and cannot get money elsewhere.

Did You Know?

When purchasing a home, car, or applying for a loan, lenders and banks will check your 3-in-1 Credit Report to help them decide whether to give you a loan or credit card. The 3-in-1 report provides the report and score for all three major credit agencies. Mortgage lenders will use your middle score to determine if you will be granted credit and at what interest rate credit will be approved.

I received a collection agency letter, what should I do?

First of all, keep your cool. It is easier to think when you have a clear head. By law, a collection agency is required to notify you in writing of its intent to collect on a debt. You in turn, by law, have 30 days to dispute the debt and/or require the collection agency to validate the alleged debt. If you look at the letter you received from the collection agency you will see this information as well as a statement indicating if the collection agency does not hear from you within 30 days, they will assume that the debt is valid.

When you request that a collection agency validate the alleged debt you owe, they must prove that you indeed are the owner of the debt before they may collect. The Fair Debt Collection Practice Act, details the actions a collection agency must take if you request debt validation. If they do not comply, the collection agency must discontinue all efforts to contact you or collect monies from you. Also, the collection agency must validate the alleged debt to your satisfaction, such as providing you copies of all statements while the account was open, and a copy of the agreement with the original creditor that gives the collection agency the right to collect the alleged debt.

Did You Know?

When you dispute derogatory items on your credit report they are temporarily not calculated into your credit score until the conclusion of the investigation, which will temporarily (for up to 30 days) increase your credit score. This does not apply to disputes of public records.

SAMPLE LETTERS

WARNING: Use these letters as examples only. You must customize them to meet your particular need. Also, if the credit bureau believes that you are using form letters they will assume that your request is frivolous and by law may refuse to investigate your dispute.

SAMPLE CEASE & DESIST LETTER FOR COLLECTION AGENCIES

YOUR NAME
YOUR ADDRESS
CITY, STATE, ZIP

VIA CERTIFIED MAIL#

Date

Collection Agency
1234 North Place
Philadelphia , SA 99299

RE: Account # ____________

Dear Debt Collection Agency:

You are hereby notified, under the provision of "The Fair Debt Collection Practices Act," to CEASE and DESIST in your efforts to collect on the above mentioned account. I choose to only deal with the original creditor of the account.

If you fail to heed this notice, I will file a formal complaint against you with the Federal Trade Commission who is responsible for enforcement, and the state Attorney General's Office.

Please give this matter the attention it deserves. Thank you.

Your signature
Your name

SAMPLE CREDIT BUREAU DISPUTE LETTER

Your Name
Your Street Address
Your City, ST 99999
SSN XXX-XX-XXXX
DOB: 1/1/00

Credit Bureau
Credit Bureau Address
Credit Bureau Land, Any State 88888

Date:

Dear (Name of Credit Bureau):

This dispute is intended as a formal complaint that you are reporting inaccurate credit information on my credit report. The Fair Credit Reporting Act states that it is the responsibility of the credit bureau to ensure that all information contained within my credit file is free from error.

The following information, therefore, needs to be verified and deleted from the report as soon as possible:

CREDITOR: acct. XXXX-XXX-XXXX-XXXX

Upon the completion of your investigation, please send me a copy of the results of your investigation, along with a copy of my updated credit report.

Sincerely,

Your Signature
Your Name

SAMPLE CREDIT BUREAU DISPUTE LETTER 2

Your Name
Your Street Address
Your City, ST 99999
SSN XXX-XX-XXXX
DOB: 1/1/00

Credit Bureau
Credit Bureau Address
Credit Bureau Land, Any State 88888

Date:

To Whom it May Concern:

Dear (Name of Credit Bureau):

Approximately a month ago, I submitted a dispute regarding inaccurate information found on my credit report. As of date, I have not received your response. According to the Fair Credit Reporting Act, if you can not verify the information in dispute within 30 days, you must remove the information from my credit file.

As previously stated, I completely disagree with the following entry in my credit file:

Creditor : acct. xxxx-xxx-xxxx-xxxx

Please send me confirmation, showing the results of your investigation. If you have not received verification, I request that the above entry be deleted from my credit record. Thank you in advance for your prompt attention to this matter.

Sincerely,

Your Signature
Your Name

SAMPLE RESPONSE TO CREDIT BUREAU FRIVOLOUS DISPUTE LETTER

Your Name
Your Street Address
Your City, ST 99999
SSN XXX-XX-XXXX
DOB: 1/1/00

Credit Bureau
Credit Bureau Address
Credit Bureau Land, Any State 88888

Date:

To Whom it May Concern:

Dear (Name of Credit Bureau Contact):

I received your letter dated _____. Thank you for your prompt response. However, I do not understand why my request to remove inaccurate information has been rejected as frivolous. I completely disagree with the following entry in my credit report.

Creditor : acct. xxxx-xxx-xxxx-xxxx

Please send me confirmation, showing the results of your investigation. I would respectfully ask that you do not tell me that my request is frivolous again. This problem is very important to me, and it warrants an investigation.

Sincerely,

Your Signature
Your Name

SAMPLE GOODWILL LETTER TO CREDITOR

Original Creditor
Original Creditor Address
City, State 9999

Date

Regarding: Account No. XXXXXXXXXXXXXX

Dear Account Manager:

I have been your customer for over_________years. During this time I have made every effort to pay my bills on time every time. Unfortunately, unforeseen circumstances caused me to be 30 days late one time in all of my _________years with your company. For that I sincerely apologize.

Now I am in the process of purchasing a home and the 30 day late notation mentioned above may preclude me from taking full advantage of the very lowest interest rates available at this time. Because this notation does not reflect my current payment status, I respectfully request that you remove this information from my credit file.

Thank you very much for your consideration.

Sincerely,

Your Signature
Your Name

SAMPLE COLLECTION VALIDATION LETTER

Your Name
Your Address
City, State 9999

Date

Regarding: Account No. XXXXXXXXXXXXXX

Dear (Name of Collection Agency):

This letter is being sent to you in response to your collection letter dated_____________. This letter serves as a dispute to your claim, in no way is it a refusal to pay. Also, this letter serves as a request for validation pursuant to the Fair Debt Collection Practices Act.

Please be advised that reporting invalidated information to major credit bureaus might constitute fraud under federal and state laws. You should also be aware that if any negative entries are placed by you on my credit report, this could result in my filing an immediate lawsuit against you and your client for Violation of the Fair Credit Reporting Act and the Fair Debt Collection Practices Act.

In the mean time and not until the conclusion of your investigation, please do not take any action that could be detrimental to any of my credit files.

To validate the debt in question, please provide me with the following:

Name and Address of Creditor
Name of Debtor
Account Number
Address of Debtor
Amount of Alleged Debt
Date it was due
Date of original delinquency or charge off
Was this Debt assigned to your collection agency or purchased?
Amount paid if debt was purchased
Commission for your collection agency if collection efforts are successful

Continued on next page

Please attach a copy of the agreement with your client that grants you the authority to collect on this alleged debt.

Please attach a copy of any signed agreement that the alleged debtor has made with alleged debt collector, wherein the alleged debtor has a contractual obligation to pay debt collector.

Please provide copies of all statements while this account was open.

Please attach any signed agreements with the alleged debtor, wherein the alleged debtor agreed to pay creditor.

Have any insurance claims been made by any creditor regarding this account?

Have any judgments been obtained by any creditor regarding this account?

Have any negative trade lines been reported to any credit reporting agencies regarding this alleged debt? If so, please list the credit reporting bureaus to whom this information was reported.

Please provide the name and address of the bonding agent for your collection agency in case legal action becomes necessary.

Please note that you are required by law to return the requested information within 30 days of your receipt of this letter. Failure to do so will make you in violation of the Fair Debt Collection Practices Act.

Please provide 30 days for processing after I have received the above requested information from you.

Thank you.

Your Signature
Your Name

SAMPLE AGREEMENT TO COMPROMISE DEBT

(Name of Creditor), referred to as CREDITOR and (Your Name), referred to as DEBTOR, agree to compromise the indebtedness as between them. CREDITOR, hereby agrees to compromise the indebtedness due the CREDITOR on the following terms and conditions:

The CREDITOR and the DEBTOR agree that the present debt due is $2,000 (Two Thousand dollars and no cents). The parties agree that the CREDITOR shall accept the sum of $1200.50 (one thousand two-hundred and 50/100 dollars) as full payment on the debt. The acceptance of the payment will serve as a complete discharge of all monies due. The payment shall be in the form of a (cashier's check , money order or a personal check)

Upon receipt of settlement of $1200.50, the creditor will notifiy all of the credit bureaus that the account is "Paid as Agreed" and request that all negative entries made regarding this account be deleted.

This compromise is expressly conditioned upon the payment being received by *(agreed upon date)*. If the DEBTOR fails to pay the compromised amount by *(agreed upon date)*, the original amount owed by the DEBTOR will be reinstated in full, and immediately due.

(Collection Agency representative)hereby declares that he is authorized to act as an agent of the credit agency.

This Agreement shall be binding upon and inure to the benefit of the parties, their successors, and assignees.

Dated:

Signature:

Max Creditor
CREDITOR

Signature

Jane Doe
DEBTOR

FAIR CREDIT REPORTING ACT

The bible says, "My people perish for the lack of knowledge." It also says, "In all your getting, get understanding."

Take some time to read this act and the others listed in this guide, so that you may exercise your right to obtain and maintain good credit and experience the benefits that come along with it.

THE FAIR CREDIT REPORTING ACT

As a public service, the staff of the Federal Trade Commission (FTC) has prepared the following complete text of the Fair Credit Reporting Act (FCRA), 15 U.S.C. § 1681 et seq. Although staff generally followed the format of the U.S. Code as published by the Government Printing Office, the format of this text does differ in minor ways from the Code (and from West's U.S. Code Annotated). For example, this version uses FCRA section numbers (§§ 601-625) in the headings. (The relevant U.S. Code citation is included with each section heading and each reference to the FCRA in the text.)

This version of the FCRA is complete as of January 7, 2002. It includes the amendments to the FCRA set forth in the Consumer Credit Reporting Reform Act of 1996 (Public Law 104-208, the Omnibus Consolidated Appropriations Act for Fiscal Year 1997, Title II, Subtitle D, Chapter 1), Section 311 of the Intelligence Authorization for Fiscal Year 1998 (Public Law 105-107), the Consumer Reporting Employment Clarification Act of 1998 (Public Law 105-347), Section 506 of the Gramm-Leach-Bliley Act (Public Law 106-102), and Sections 358(g) and 505(c) of the Uniting and Strengthening America by Providing Appropriate Tools Required to Intercept and Obstruct Terrorism Act of 2001 (USA PATRIOT Act) (Public Law 107-56).

TABLE OF CONTENTS

§ 601. Short title

This title may be cited as the Fair Credit Reporting Act.

§ 602. Congressional findings and statement of purpose [15 U.S.C. § 1681]

(a) Accuracy and fairness of credit reporting. The Congress makes the following findings:

(1) The banking system is dependent upon fair and accurate credit reporting. Inaccurate credit reports directly impair the efficiency of the banking system, and unfair credit reporting methods undermine the public confidence which is essential to the continued functioning of the banking system.

(2) An elaborate mechanism has been developed for investigating and evaluating the credit worthiness, credit standing, credit capacity, character, and general reputation of consumers.

(3) Consumer reporting agencies have assumed a vital role in assembling and evaluating consumer credit and other information on consumers.

(4) There is a need to insure that consumer reporting agencies exercise their grave responsibilities with fairness, impartiality, and a respect for the consumer's right to privacy.

(b) Reasonable procedures. It is the purpose of this title to require that consumer reporting agencies adopt reasonable procedures for meeting the needs of commerce for consumer credit, personnel, insurance, and other information in a manner which is fair and equitable to the consumer, with regard to the confidentiality, accuracy, relevancy, and proper utilization of such information in accordance with the requirements of this title.

§ 603. Definitions; rules of construction [15 U.S.C. § 1681a]

(a) Definitions and rules of construction set forth in this section are applicable for the purposes of this title.

(b) The term "person" means any individual, partnership, corporation, trust, estate, cooperative, association, government or governmental subdivision or agency, or other entity.

(c) The term "consumer" means an individual.

(d) Consumer report.

(1) In general. The term "consumer report" means any written, oral, or other communication of any information by a consumer reporting agency bearing on a consumer's credit worthiness, credit standing, credit capacity, character, general reputation, personal characteristics, or mode of living which is used or expected to be used or collected in whole or in part for the purpose of serving as a factor in establishing the consumer's eligibility for

(A) credit or insurance to be used primarily for personal, family, or household purposes;

(B) employment purposes; or

(C) any other purpose authorized under section 604 [§ 1681b].

(2) Exclusions. The term "consumer report" does not include

(A) any

(i) report containing information solely as to transactions or experiences between the consumer and the person making the report;

(ii) communication of that information among persons related by common ownership or affiliated by corporate control; or

(iii) communication of other information among persons related by common ownership or affiliated by corporate control, if it is clearly and conspicuously disclosed to the consumer that the information may be communicated

among such persons and the consumer is given the opportunity, before the time that the information is initially communicated, to direct that such information not be communicated among such persons;
(B) any authorization or approval of a specific extension of credit directly or indirectly by the issuer of a credit card or similar device;
(C) any report in which a person who has been requested by a third party to make a specific extension of credit directly or indirectly to a consumer conveys his or her decision with respect to such request, if the third party advises the consumer of the name and address of the person to whom the request was made, and such person makes the disclosures to the consumer required under section 615 [§ 1681m]; or
(D) a communication described in subsection (o).
(e) The term "investigative consumer report" means a consumer report or portion thereof in which information on a consumer's character, general reputation, personal characteristics, or mode of living is obtained through personal interviews with neighbors, friends, or associates of the consumer reported on or with others with whom he is acquainted or who may have knowledge concerning any such items of information. However, such information shall not include specific factual information on a consumer's credit record obtained directly from a creditor of the consumer or from a consumer reporting agency when such information was obtained directly from a creditor of the consumer or from the consumer.
(f) The term "consumer reporting agency" means any person which, for monetary fees, dues, or on a cooperative nonprofit basis, regularly engages in whole or in part in the practice of assembling or evaluating consumer credit information or other information on consumers for the purpose of furnishing consumer reports to third parties, and which uses any means or facility of interstate commerce for the purpose of preparing or furnishing consumer reports.
(g) The term "file," when used in connection with information on any consumer, means all of the information on that consumer recorded and retained by a consumer reporting agency regardless of how the information is stored.
(h) The term "employment purposes" when used in connection with a consumer report means a report used for the purpose of evaluating a consumer for employment, promotion, reassignment or retention as an employee.
(i) The term "medical information" means information or records obtained, with the consent of the individual to whom it relates, from licensed physicians or medical practitioners, hospitals, clinics, or other medical or medically related facilities.
(j) Definitions relating to child support obligations.
(1) Overdue support. The term "overdue support" has the meaning given to such term in section 666(e) of title 42 [Social Security Act, 42 U.S.C. § 666(e)].
(2) State or local child support enforcement agency. The term "State or local child support enforcement agency" means a State or local agency which administers a State or local program for establishing and enforcing child support obligations.
(k) Adverse action.
(1) Actions included. The term "adverse action"
(A) has the same meaning as in section 701(d)(6) of the Equal Credit Opportunity Act; and
(B) means
(i) a denial or cancellation of, an increase in any charge for, or a reduction or other adverse or unfavorable change in the terms of coverage or amount of, any insurance, existing or applied for, in connection with the underwriting of

insurance;
(ii) a denial of employment or any other decision for employment purposes that adversely affects any current or prospective employee;
(iii) a denial or cancellation of, an increase in any charge for, or any other adverse or unfavorable change in the terms of, any license or benefit described in section 604(a)(3)(D) [§ 1681b]; and
(iv) an action taken or determination that is
(I) made in connection with an application that was made by, or a transaction that was initiated by, any consumer, or in connection with a review of an account under section 604(a)(3)(F)(ii)[§ 1681b]; and
(II) adverse to the interests of the consumer.
(2) Applicable findings, decisions, commentary, and orders. For purposes of any determination of whether an action is an adverse action under paragraph (1)(A), all appropriate final findings, decisions, commentary, and orders issued under section 701(d)(6) of the Equal Credit Opportunity Act by the Board of Governors of the Federal Reserve System or any court shall apply.
(l) Firm offer of credit or insurance. The term "firm offer of credit or insurance" means any offer of credit or insurance to a consumer that will be honored if the consumer is determined, based on information in a consumer report on the consumer, to meet the specific criteria used to select the consumer for the offer, except that the offer may be further conditioned on one or more of the following:
(1) The consumer being determined, based on information in the consumer's application for the credit or insurance, to meet specific criteria bearing on credit worthiness or insurability, as applicable, that are established
(A) before selection of the consumer for the offer; and
(B) for the purpose of determining whether to extend credit or insurance pursuant to the offer.
(2) Verification
(A) that the consumer continues to meet the specific criteria used to select the consumer for the offer, by using information in a consumer report on the consumer, information in the consumer's application for the credit or insurance, or other information bearing on the credit worthiness or insurability of the consumer; or
(B) of the information in the consumer's application for the credit or insurance, to determine that the consumer meets the specific criteria bearing on credit worthiness or insurability.
(3) The consumer furnishing any collateral that is a requirement for the extension of the credit or insurance that was
(A) established before selection of the consumer for the offer of credit or insurance; and
(B) disclosed to the consumer in the offer of credit or insurance.
(m) Credit or insurance transaction that is not initiated by the consumer. The term"credit or insurance transaction that is not initiated by the consumer" does not include the use of a consumer report by a person with which the consumer has an account or insurance policy, for purposes of
(1) reviewing the account or insurance policy; or
(2) collecting the account.
(n) State. The term "State" means any State, the Commonwealth of Puerto Rico, the District of Columbia, and any territory or possession of the United States.
(o) Excluded communications. A communication is described in this subsection if it is a communication
(1) that, but for subsection (d)(2)(D), would be an investigative consumer report;
(2) that is made to a prospective employer for the purpose of
(A) procuring an employee for the employer; or

(B) procuring an opportunity for a natural person to work for the employer;
(3) that is made by a person who regularly performs such procurement;
(4) that is not used by any person for any purpose other than a purpose described in subparagraph (A) or (B) of paragraph (2); and
(5) with respect to which
(A) the consumer who is the subject of the communication
(i) consents orally or in writing to the nature and scope of the communication, before the collection of any information for the purpose of making the communication;
(ii) consents orally or in writing to the making of the communication to a prospective employer, before the making of the communication; and
(iii) in the case of consent under clause (i) or (ii) given orally, is provided written confirmation of that consent by the person making the communication, not later than 3 business days after the receipt of the consent by that person;
(B) the person who makes the communication does not, for the purpose of making the communication, make any inquiry that if made by a prospective employer of the consumer who is the subject of the communication would violate any applicable Federal or State equal employment opportunity law or regulation; and
(C) the person who makes the communication
(i) discloses in writing to the consumer who is the subject of the communication, not later than 5 business days after receiving any request from the consumer for such disclosure, the nature and substance of all information in the consumer's file at the time of the request, except that the sources of any information that is acquired solely for use in making the communication and is actually used for no other purpose, need not be disclosed other than under appropriate discovery procedures in any court of competent jurisdiction in which an action is brought; and
(ii) notifies the consumer who is the subject of the communication, in writing, of the consumer's right to request the information described in clause (i).
(p) Consumer reporting agency that compiles and maintains files on consumers on a nationwide basis. The term "consumer reporting agency that compiles and maintains files on consumers on a nationwide basis" means a consumer reporting agency that regularly engages in the practice of assembling or evaluating, and maintaining, for the purpose of furnishing consumer reports to third parties bearing on a consumer's credit worthiness, credit standing, or credit capacity, each of the following regarding consumers residing nationwide:
(1) Public record information.
(2) Credit account information from persons who furnish that information regularly and in the ordinary course of business.

§ 604. Permissible purposes of consumer reports [15 U.S.C. § 1681b]

(a) In general. Subject to subsection (c), any consumer reporting agency may furnish a consumer report under the following circumstances and no other:
(1) In response to the order of a court having jurisdiction to issue such an order, or a subpoena issued in connection with proceedings before a Federal grand jury.
(2) In accordance with the written instructions of the consumer to whom it relates.
(3) To a person which it has reason to believe
(A) intends to use the information in connection with a credit transaction involving the consumer on whom the

information is to be furnished and involving the extension of credit to, or review or collection of an account of, the consumer; or

(B) intends to use the information for employment purposes; or

(C) intends to use the information in connection with the underwriting of insurance involving the consumer; or

(D) intends to use the information in connection with a determination of the consumer's eligibility for a license or other benefit granted by a governmental instrumentality required by law to consider an applicant's financial responsibility or status; or

(E) intends to use the information, as a potential investor or servicer, or current insurer, in connection with a valuation of, or an assessment of the credit or prepayment risks associated with, an existing credit obligation; or

(F) otherwise has a legitimate business need for the information

(i) in connection with a business transaction that is initiated by the consumer; or

(ii) to review an account to determine whether the consumer continues to meet the terms of the account.

(4) In response to a request by the head of a State or local child support enforcement agency (or a State or local government official authorized by the head of such an agency), if the person making the request certifies to the consumer reporting agency that

(A) the consumer report is needed for the purpose of establishing an individual's capacity to make child support payments or determining the appropriate level of such payments;

(B) the paternity of the consumer for the child to which the obligation relates has been established or acknowledged by the consumer in accordance with State laws under which the obligation arises (if required by those laws);

(C) the person has provided at least 10 days' prior notice to the consumer whose report is requested, by certified or registered mail to the last known address of the consumer, that the report will be requested; and

(D) the consumer report will be kept confidential, will be used solely for a purpose described in subparagraph (A), and will not be used in connection with any other civil, administrative, or criminal proceeding, or for any other purpose.

(5) To an agency administering a State plan under Section 454 of the Social Security Act (42 U.S.C. § 654) for use to set an initial or modified child support award.

(b) Conditions for furnishing and using consumer reports for employment purposes.

(1) Certification from user. A consumer reporting agency may furnish a consumer report for employment purposes only if

(A) the person who obtains such report from the agency certifies to the agency that

(i) the person has complied with paragraph (2) with respect to the consumer report, and the person will comply with paragraph (3) with respect to the consumer report if paragraph (3) becomes applicable; and

(ii) information from the consumer report will not be used in violation of any applicable Federal or State equal employment opportunity law or regulation; and

(B) the consumer reporting agency provides with the report, or has previously provided, a summary of the consumer's rights under this title, as prescribed by the Federal Trade Commission under section 609(c)(3) [§ 1681g].

(2) Disclosure to consumer.

(A) In general. Except as provided in subparagraph (B), a person may not procure a consumer report, or cause a consumer report to be procured, for employment purposes with respect to any consumer, unless—

(i) a clear and conspicuous disclosure has been made in writing to the consumer at any time before the report is procured or caused to be procured, in a document that consists solely of the disclosure, that a consumer report may be obtained for employment purposes; and

(ii) the consumer has authorized in writing (which authorization may be made on the document referred to in clause (i)) the procurement of the report by that person.

(B) Application by mail, telephone, computer, or other similar means. If a consumer described in subparagraph (C) applies for employment by mail, telephone, computer, or other similar means, at any time before a consumer report is procured or caused to be procured in connection with that application—

(i) the person who procures the consumer report on the consumer for employment purposes shall provide to the consumer, by oral, written, or electronic means, notice that a consumer report may be obtained for employment purposes, and a summary of the consumer's rights under section 615(a)(3); and

(ii) the consumer shall have consented, orally, in writing, or electronically to the procurement of the report by that person.

(C) Scope. Subparagraph (B) shall apply to a person procuring a consumer report on a consumer in connection with the consumer's application for employment only if—

(i) the consumer is applying for a position over which the Secretary of Transportation has the power to establish qualifications and maximum hours of service pursuant to the provisions of section 31502 of title 49, or a position subject to safety regulation by a State transportation agency; and

(ii) as of the time at which the person procures the report or causes the report to be procured the only interaction between the consumer and the person in connection with that employment application has been by mail, telephone, computer, or other similar means.

(3) Conditions on use for adverse actions.

(A) In general. Except as provided in subparagraph (B), in using a consumer report for employment purposes, before taking any adverse action based in whole or in part on the report, the person intending to take such adverse action shall provide to the consumer to whom the report relates—

(i) a copy of the report; and

(ii) a description in writing of the rights of the consumer under this title, as prescribed by the Federal Trade Commission under section 609(c)(3).

(B) Application by mail, telephone, computer, or other similar means.

(i) If a consumer described in subparagraph (C) applies for employment by mail, telephone, computer, or other similar means, and if a person who has procured a consumer report on the consumer for employment purposes takes adverse action on the employment application based in whole or in part on the report, then the person must provide to the consumer to whom the report relates, in lieu of the notices required under subparagraph (A) of this section and under section 615(a), within 3 business days of taking such action, an oral, written or electronic notification—

(I) that adverse action has been taken based in whole or in part on a consumer report received from a consumer reporting agency;

(II) of the name, address and telephone number of the consumer reporting agency that furnished the consumer report (including a toll-free telephone number established by the agency if the agency compiles and maintains files

on consumers on a nationwide basis);
(III) that the consumer reporting agency did not make the decision to take the adverse action and is unable to provide to the consumer the specific reasons why the adverse action was taken; and
(IV) that the consumer may, upon providing proper identification, request a free copy of a report and may dispute with the consumer reporting agency the accuracy or completeness of any information in a report.
(ii) If, under clause (B)(i)(IV), the consumer requests a copy of a consumer report from the person who procured the report, then, within 3 business days of receiving the consumer's request, together with proper identification, the person must send or provide to the consumer a copy of a report and a copy of the consumer's rights as prescribed by the Federal Trade Commission under section 609(c)(3).
(C) Scope. Subparagraph (B) shall apply to a person procuring a consumer report on a consumer in connection with the consumer's application for employment only if—
(i) the consumer is applying for a position over which the Secretary of Transportation has the power to establish qualifications and maximum hours of service pursuant to the provisions of section 31502 of title 49, or a position subject to safety regulation by a State transportation agency; and
(ii) as of the time at which the person procures the report or causes the report to be procured the only interaction between the consumer and the person in connection with that employment application has been by mail, telephone, computer, or other similar means.
(4) Exception for national security investigations.
(A) In general. In the case of an agency or department of the United States Government which seeks to obtain and use a consumer report for employment purposes, paragraph (3) shall not apply to any adverse action by such agency or department which is based in part on such consumer report, if the head of such agency or department makes a written finding that—
(i) the consumer report is relevant to a national security investigation of such agency or department;
(ii) the investigation is within the jurisdiction of such agency or department;
(iii) there is reason to believe that compliance with paragraph (3) will—
(I) endanger the life or physical safety of any person;
(II) result in flight from prosecution;
(III) result in the destruction of, or tampering with, evidence relevant to the investigation;
(IV) result in the intimidation of a potential witness relevant to the investigation;
(V) result in the compromise of classified information; or
(VI) otherwise seriously jeopardize or unduly delay the investigation or another official proceeding.
(B) Notification of consumer upon conclusion of investigation. Upon the conclusion of a national security investigation described in subparagraph (A), or upon the determination that the exception under subparagraph (A) is no longer required for the reasons set forth in such subparagraph, the official exercising the authority in such subparagraph shall provide to the consumer who is the subject of the consumer report with regard to which such finding was made—
(i) a copy of such consumer report with any classified information redacted as necessary;
(ii) notice of any adverse action which is based, in part, on the consumer report; and
(iii) the identification with reasonable specificity of the nature of the investigation for which the consumer report was

sought.

(C) Delegation by head of agency or department. For purposes of subparagraphs (A) and (B), the head of any agency or department of the United States Government may delegate his or her authorities under this paragraph to an official of such agency or department who has personnel security responsibilities and is a member of the Senior Executive Service or equivalent civilian or military rank.

(D) Report to the congress. Not later than January 31 of each year, the head of each agency and department of the United States Government that exercised authority under this paragraph during the preceding year shall submit a report to the Congress on the number of times the department or agency exercised such authority during the year.

(E) Definitions. For purposes of this paragraph, the following definitions shall apply:

(i) Classified information. The term 'classified information' means information that is protected from unauthorized disclosure under Executive Order No. 12958 or successor orders.

(ii) National security investigation. The term 'national security investigation' means any official inquiry by an agency or department of the United States Government to determine the eligibility of a consumer to receive access or continued access to classified information or to determine whether classified information has been lost or compromised.

(c) Furnishing reports in connection with credit or insurance transactions that are not initiated by the consumer.

(1) In general. A consumer reporting agency may furnish a consumer report relating to any consumer pursuant to subparagraph (A) or (C) of subsection (a)(3) in connection with any credit or insurance transaction that is not initiated by the consumer only if

(A) the consumer authorizes the agency to provide such report to such person; or

(B) (i) the transaction consists of a firm offer of credit or insurance;

(ii) the consumer reporting agency has complied with subsection (e); and

(iii) there is not in effect an election by the consumer, made in accordance with subsection (e), to have the consumer's name and address excluded from lists of names provided by the agency pursuant to this paragraph.

(2) Limits on information received under paragraph (1)(B). A person may receive pursuant to paragraph (1)(B) only

(A) the name and address of a consumer;

(B) an identifier that is not unique to the consumer and that is used by the person solely for the purpose of verifying the identity of the consumer; and

(C) other information pertaining to a consumer that does not identify the relationship or experience of the consumer with respect to a particular creditor or other entity.

(3) Information regarding inquiries. Except as provided in section 609(a)(5) [§ 1681g], a consumer reporting agency shall not furnish to any person a record of inquiries in connection with a credit or insurance transaction that is not initiated by a consumer.

(d) Reserved.

(e) Election of consumer to be excluded from lists.

(1) In general. A consumer may elect to have the consumer's name and address excluded from any list provided by a consumer reporting agency under subsection (c)(1)(B) in connection with a credit or insurance transaction that is not initiated by the consumer, by notifying the agency in accordance with paragraph (2) that the consumer does not consent to any use of a consumer report relating to the consumer in connection with any credit or insurance

transaction that is not initiated by the consumer.

(2) Manner of notification. A consumer shall notify a consumer reporting agency under paragraph (1)

(A) through the notification system maintained by the agency under paragraph (5); or

(B) by submitting to the agency a signed notice of election form issued by the agency for purposes of this subparagraph.

(3) Response of agency after notification through system. Upon receipt of notification of the election of a consumer under paragraph (1) through the notification system maintained by the agency under paragraph (5), a consumer reporting agency shall

(A) inform the consumer that the election is effective only for the 2-year period following the election if the consumer does not submit to the agency a signed notice of election form issued by the agency for purposes of paragraph (2)(B); and

(B) provide to the consumer a notice of election form, if requested by the consumer, not later than 5 business days after receipt of the notification of the election through the system established under paragraph (5), in the case of a request made at the time the consumer provides notification through the system.

(4) Effectiveness of election. An election of a consumer under paragraph (1)

(A) shall be effective with respect to a consumer reporting agency beginning 5 business days after the date on which the consumer notifies the agency in accordance with paragraph (2);

(B) shall be effective with respect to a consumer reporting agency

(i) subject to subparagraph (C), during the 2-year period beginning 5 business days after the date on which the consumer notifies the agency of the election, in the case of an election for which a consumer notifies the agency only in accordance with paragraph (2)(A); or

(ii) until the consumer notifies the agency under subparagraph (C), in the case of an election for which a consumer notifies the agency in accordance with paragraph (2)(B);

(C) shall not be effective after the date on which the consumer notifies the agency, through the notification system established by the agency under paragraph (5), that the election is no longer effective; and

(D) shall be effective with respect to each affiliate of the agency.

(5) Notification system.

(A) In general. Each consumer reporting agency that, under subsection (c)(1)(B), furnishes a consumer report in connection with a credit or insurance transaction that is not initiated by a consumer, shall

(i) establish and maintain a notification system, including a toll-free telephone number, which permits any consumer whose consumer report is maintained by the agency to notify the agency, with appropriate identification, of the consumer's election to have the consumer's name and address excluded from any such list of names and addresses provided by the agency for such a transaction; and

(ii) publish by not later than 365 days after the date of enactment of the Consumer Credit Reporting Reform Act of 1996, and not less than annually thereafter, in a publication of general circulation in the area served by the agency

(I) a notification that information in consumer files maintained by the agency may be used in connection with such transactions; and

(II) the address and toll-free telephone number for consumers to use to notify the agency of the consumer's election under clause (I).

(B) Establishment and maintenance as compliance. Establishment and maintenance of a notification system (including a toll-free telephone number) and publication by a consumer reporting agency on the agency's own behalf and on behalf of any of its affiliates in accordance with this paragraph is deemed to be compliance with this paragraph by each of those affiliates.

(6) Notification system by agencies that operate nationwide. Each consumer reporting agency that compiles and maintains files on consumers on a nationwide basis shall establish and maintain a notification system for purposes of paragraph (5) jointly with other such consumer reporting agencies.

(f) Certain use or obtaining of information prohibited. A person shall not use or obtain a consumer report for any purpose unless

(1) the consumer report is obtained for a purpose for which the consumer report is authorized to be furnished under this section; and

(2) the purpose is certified in accordance with section 607 [§ 1681e] by a prospective user of the report through a general or specific certification.

(g) Furnishing reports containing medical information. A consumer reporting agency shall not furnish for employment purposes, or in connection with a credit or insurance transaction, a consumer report that contains medical information about a consumer, unless the consumer consents to the furnishing of the report.

§ 605. Requirements relating to information contained in consumer reports [15 U.S.C. § 1681c]

(a) Information excluded from consumer reports. Except as authorized under subsection (b) of this section, no consumer reporting agency may make any consumer report containing any of the following items of information:

(1) Cases under title 11 [United States Code] or under the Bankruptcy Act that, from the date of entry of the order for relief or the date of adjudication, as the case may be, antedate the report by more than 10 years.

(2) Civil suits, civil judgments, and records of arrest that from date of entry, antedate the report by more than seven years or until the governing statute of limitations has expired, whichever is the longer period.

(3) Paid tax liens which, from date of payment, antedate the report by more than seven years.

(4) Accounts placed for collection or charged to profit and loss which antedate the report by more than seven years.[(1)]

(5) Any other adverse item of information, other than records of convictions of crimes which antedates the report by more than seven years.[1]

(b) Exempted cases. The provisions of subsection (a) of this section are not applicable in the case of any consumer credit report to be used in connection with

(1) a credit transaction involving, or which may reasonably be expected to involve, a principal amount of $150,000 or more;

(2) the underwriting of life insurance involving, or which may reasonably be expected to involve, a face amount of $150,000 or more; or

(3) the employment of any individual at an annual salary which equals, or which may reasonably be expected to equal $75,000, or more.

(c) Running of reporting period.

(1) In general. The 7-year period referred to in paragraphs (4) and (6)[(2)] of subsection (a) shall begin, with respect to any delinquent account that is placed for collection (internally or by referral to a third party, whichever is earlier), charged to profit and loss, or subjected to any similar action, upon the expiration of the 180-day period beginning on

the date of the commencement of the delinquency which immediately preceded the collection activity, charge to profit and loss, or similar action.

(2) Effective date. Paragraph (1) shall apply only to items of information added to the file of a consumer on or after the date that is 455 days after the date of enactment of the Consumer Credit Reporting Reform Act of 1996.

(d) Information required to be disclosed. Any consumer reporting agency that furnishes a consumer report that contains information regarding any case involving the consumer that arises under title 11, United States Code, shall include in the report an identification of the chapter of such title 11 under which such case arises if provided by the source of the information. If any case arising or filed under title 11, United States Code, is withdrawn by the consumer before a final judgment, the consumer reporting agency shall include in the report that such case or filing was withdrawn upon receipt of documentation certifying such withdrawal.

(e) Indication of closure of account by consumer. If a consumer reporting agency is notified pursuant to section 623(a)(4) [§ 1681s-2] that a credit account of a consumer was voluntarily closed by the consumer, the agency shall indicate that fact in any consumer report that includes information related to the account.

(f) Indication of dispute by consumer. If a consumer reporting agency is notified pursuant to section 623(a)(3) [§ 1681s-2] that information regarding a consumer who was furnished to the agency is disputed by the consumer, the agency shall indicate that fact in each consumer report that includes the disputed information.

§ 606. Disclosure of investigative consumer reports [15 U.S.C. § 1681d]

(a) Disclosure of fact of preparation. A person may not procure or cause to be prepared an investigative consumer report on any consumer unless

(1) it is clearly and accurately disclosed to the consumer that an investigative consumer report including information as to his character, general reputation, personal characteristics and mode of living, whichever are applicable, may be made, and such disclosure

(A) is made in a writing mailed, or otherwise delivered, to the consumer, not later than three days after the date on which the report was first requested, and

(B) includes a statement informing the consumer of his right to request the additional disclosures provided for under subsection (b) of this section and the written summary of the rights of the consumer prepared pursuant to section 609(c) [§ 1681g]; and

(2) the person certifies or has certified to the consumer reporting agency that

(A) the person has made the disclosures to the consumer required by paragraph (1); and

(B) the person will comply with subsection (b).

(b) Disclosure on request of nature and scope of investigation. Any person who procures or causes to be prepared an investigative consumer report on any consumer shall, upon written request made by the consumer within a reasonable period of time after the receipt by him of the disclosure required by subsection (a)(1) of this section, make a complete and accurate disclosure of the nature and scope of the investigation requested. This disclosure shall be made in a writing mailed, or otherwise delivered, to the consumer not later than five days after the date on which the request for such disclosure was received from the consumer or such report was first requested, whichever is the later.

(c) Limitation on liability upon showing of reasonable procedures for compliance with provisions. No person may be held liable for any violation of subsection (a) or (b) of this section if he shows by a preponderance of the evidence that at the time of the violation he maintained reasonable procedures to assure compliance with subsection (a) or (b) of this section.

(d) Prohibitions.

(1) Certification. A consumer reporting agency shall not prepare or furnish investigative consumer report unless the agency has received a certification under subsection (a)(2) from the person who requested the report.

(2) Inquiries. A consumer reporting agency shall not make an inquiry for the purpose of preparing an investigative consumer report on a consumer for employment purposes if the making of the inquiry by an employer or prospective employer of the consumer would violate any applicable Federal or State equal employment opportunity law or regulation.

(3) Certain public record information. Except as otherwise provided in section 613 [§ 1681k], a consumer reporting agency shall not furnish an investigative consumer report that includes information that is a matter of public record and that relates to an arrest, indictment, conviction, civil judicial action, tax lien, or outstanding judgment, unless the agency has verified the accuracy of the information during the 30-day period ending on the date on which the report is furnished.

(4) Certain adverse information. A consumer reporting agency shall not prepare or furnish an investigative consumer report on a consumer that contains information that is adverse to the interest of the consumer and that is obtained through a personal interview with a neighbor, friend, or associate of the consumer or with another person with whom the consumer is acquainted or who has knowledge of such item of information, unless

(A) the agency has followed reasonable procedures to obtain confirmation of the information, from an additional source that has independent and direct knowledge of the information; or

(B) the person interviewed is the best possible source of the information.

§ 607. Compliance procedures [15 U.S.C. § 1681e]

(a) Identity and purposes of credit users. Every consumer reporting agency shall maintain reasonable procedures designed to avoid violations of section 605 [§ 1681c] and to limit the furnishing of consumer reports to the purposes listed under section 604 [§ 1681b] of this title. These procedures shall require that prospective users of the information identify themselves, certify the purposes for which the information is sought, and certify that the information will be used for no other purpose. Every consumer reporting agency shall make a reasonable effort to verify the identity of a new prospective user and the uses certified by such prospective user prior to furnishing such user a consumer report. No consumer reporting agency may furnish a consumer report to any person if it has reasonable grounds for believing that the consumer report will not be used for a purpose listed in section 604 [§ 1681b] of this title.

(b) Accuracy of report. Whenever a consumer reporting agency prepares a consumer report it shall follow reasonable procedures to assure maximum possible accuracy of the information concerning the individual about whom the report relates.

(c) Disclosure of consumer reports by users allowed. A consumer reporting agency may not prohibit a user of a consumer report furnished by the agency on a consumer from disclosing the contents of the report to the consumer, if adverse action against the consumer has been taken by the user based in whole or in part on the report.

(d) Notice to users and furnishers of information.

(1) Notice requirement. A consumer reporting agency shall provide to any person

(A) who regularly and in the ordinary course of business furnishes information to the agency with respect to any consumer; or

(B) to whom a consumer report is provided by the agency;
a notice of such person's responsibilities under this title.
(2) Content of notice. The Federal Trade Commission shall prescribe the content of notices under paragraph (1), and a consumer reporting agency shall be in compliance with this subsection if it provides a notice under paragraph (1) that is substantially similar to the Federal Trade Commission prescription under this paragraph.
(e) Procurement of consumer report for resale.
(1) Disclosure. A person may not procure a consumer report for purposes of reselling the report (or any information in the report) unless the person discloses to the consumer reporting agency that originally furnishes the report
(A) the identity of the end-user of the report (or information); and
(B) each permissible purpose under section 604 [§ 1681b] for which the report is furnished to the end-user of the report (or information).
(2) Responsibilities of procurers for resale. A person who procures a consumer report for purposes of reselling the report (or any information in the report) shall
(A) establish and comply with reasonable procedures designed to ensure that the report (or information) is resold by the person only for a purpose for which the report may be furnished under section 604 [§ 1681b], including by requiring that each person to which the report (or information) is resold and that resells or provides the report (or information) to any other person
(i) identifies each end user of the resold report (or information);
(ii) certifies each purpose for which the report (or information) will be used; and
(iii) certifies that the report (or information) will be used for no other purpose; and
(B) before reselling the report, make reasonable efforts to verify the identifications and certifications made under subparagraph (A).
(3) Resale of consumer report to a federal agency or department. Notwithstanding paragraph (1) or (2), a person who procures a consumer report for purposes of reselling the report (or any information in the report) shall not disclose the identity of the end-user of the report under paragraph (1) or (2) if—
(A) the end user is an agency or department of the United States Government which procures the report from the person for purposes of determining the eligibility of the consumer concerned to receive access or continued access to classified information (as defined in section 604(b)(4)(E)(i)); and
(B) the agency or department certifies in writing to the person reselling the report that nondisclosure is necessary to protect classified information or the safety of persons employed by or contracting with, or undergoing investigation for work or contracting with the agency or department.
§ 608. Disclosures to governmental agencies [15 U.S.C. § 1681f]
Notwithstanding the provisions of section 604 [§ 1681b] of this title, a consumer reporting agency may furnish identifying information respecting any consumer, limited to his name, address, former addresses, places of employment, or former places of employment, to a governmental agency.
§ 609. Disclosures to consumers [15 U.S.C. § 1681g]
(a) Information on file; sources; report recipients. Every consumer reporting agency shall, upon request, and subject to 610(a)(1) [§ 1681h], clearly and accurately disclose to the consumer:
(1) All information in the consumer's file at the time of the request, except that nothing in this paragraph shall be

construed to require a consumer reporting agency to disclose to a consumer any information concerning credit scores or any other risk scores or predictors relating to the consumer.

(2) The sources of the information; except that the sources of information acquired solely for use in preparing an investigative consumer report and actually used for no other purpose need not be disclosed: Provided, That in the event an action is brought under this title, such sources shall be available to the plaintiff under appropriate discovery procedures in the court in which the action is brought.

(3)(A) Identification of each person (including each end-user identified under section 607(e)(1) [§ 1681e]) that procured a consumer report

(i) for employment purposes, during the 2-year period preceding the date on which the request is made; or

(ii) for any other purpose, during the 1-year period preceding the date on which the request is made.

(B) An identification of a person under subparagraph (A) shall include

(i) the name of the person or, if applicable, the trade name (written in full) under which such person conducts business; and

(ii) upon request of the consumer, the address and telephone number of the person.

(C) Subparagraph (A) does not apply if—

(i) the end user is an agency or department of the United States Government that procures the report from the person for purposes of determining the eligibility of the consumer to whom the report relates to receive access or continued access to classified information (as defined in section 604(b)(4)(E)(i)); and

(ii) the head of the agency or department makes a written finding as prescribed under section 604(b)(4)(A).

(4) The dates, original payees, and amounts of any checks upon which is based any adverse characterization of the consumer, included in the file at the time of the disclosure.

(5) A record of all inquiries received by the agency during the 1-year period preceding the request that identified the consumer in connection with a credit or insurance transaction that was not initiated by the consumer.

(b) Exempt information. The requirements of subsection (a) of this section respecting the disclosure of sources of information and the recipients of consumer reports do not apply to information received or consumer reports furnished prior to the effective date of this title except to the extent that the matter involved is contained in the files of the consumer reporting agency on that date.

(c) Summary of rights required to be included with disclosure.

(1) Summary of rights. A consumer reporting agency shall provide to a consumer, with each written disclosure by the agency to the consumer under this section

(A) a written summary of all of the rights that the consumer has under this title; and

(B) in the case of a consumer reporting agency that compiles and maintains files on consumers on a nationwide basis, a toll-free telephone number established by the agency, at which personnel are accessible to consumers during normal business hours.

(2) Specific items required to be included. The summary of rights required under paragraph (1) shall include

(A) a brief description of this title and all rights of consumers under this title;

(B) an explanation of how the consumer may exercise the rights of the consumer under this title;
(C) a list of all Federal agencies responsible for enforcing any provision of this title and the address and any appropriate phone number of each such agency, in a form that will assist the consumer in selecting the appropriate agency;
(D) a statement that the consumer may have additional rights under State law and that the consumer may wish to contact a State or local consumer protection agency or a State attorney general to learn of those rights; and
(E) a statement that a consumer reporting agency is not required to remove accurate derogatory information from a consumer's file, unless the information is outdated under section 605 [§ 1681c] or cannot be verified.
(3) Form of summary of rights. For purposes of this subsection and any disclosure by a consumer reporting agency required under this title with respect to consumers' rights, the Federal Trade Commission (after consultation with each Federal agency referred to in section 621(b) [§ 1681s]) shall prescribe the form and content of any such disclosure of the rights of consumers required under this title. A consumer reporting agency shall be in compliance with this subsection if it provides disclosures under paragraph (1) that are substantially similar to the Federal Trade Commission prescription under this paragraph.
(4) Effectiveness. No disclosures shall be required under this subsection until the date on which the Federal Trade Commission prescribes the form and content of such disclosures under paragraph (3).
§ 610. Conditions and form of disclosure to consumers [15 U.S.C. § 1681h]
(a) In general.
(1) Proper identification. A consumer reporting agency shall require, as a condition of making the disclosures required under section 609 [§ 1681g], that the consumer furnish proper identification.
(2) Disclosure in writing. Except as provided in subsection (b), the disclosures required to be made under section 609 [§ 1681g] shall be provided under that section in writing.
(b) Other forms of disclosure.
(1) In general. If authorized by a consumer, a consumer reporting agency may make the disclosures required under 609 [§ 1681g]
(A) other than in writing; and
(B) in such form as may be
(i) specified by the consumer in accordance with paragraph (2); and
(ii) available from the agency.
(2) Form. A consumer may specify pursuant to paragraph (1) that disclosures under section 609 [§ 1681g] shall be made
(A) in person, upon the appearance of the consumer at the place of business of the consumer reporting agency where disclosures are regularly provided, during normal business hours, and on reasonable notice;
(B) by telephone, if the consumer has made a written request for disclosure by telephone;
(C) by electronic means, if available from the agency; or
(D) by any other reasonable means that is available from the agency.

(c) Trained personnel. Any consumer reporting agency shall provide trained personnel to explain to the consumer any information furnished to him pursuant to section 609 [§ 1681g] of this title.

(d) Persons accompanying consumer. The consumer shall be permitted to be accompanied by one other person of his choosing, who shall furnish reasonable identification. A consumer reporting agency may require the consumer to furnish a written statement granting permission to the consumer reporting agency to discuss the consumer's file in such person's presence.

(e) Limitation of liability. Except as provided in sections 616 and 617 [§§ 1681n and 1681o] of this title, no consumer may bring any action or proceeding in the nature of defamation, invasion of privacy, or negligence with respect to the reporting of information against any consumer reporting agency, any user of information, or any person who furnishes information to a consumer reporting agency, based on information disclosed pursuant to section 609, 610, or 615 [§§ 1681g, 1681h, or 1681m] of this title or based on information disclosed by a user of a consumer report to or for a consumer against whom the user has taken adverse action, based in whole or in part on the report, except as to false information furnished with malice or willful intent to injure such consumer.

§ 611. Procedure in case of disputed accuracy [15 U.S.C. § 1681i]

(a) Reinvestigations of disputed information.

(1) Reinvestigation required.

(A) In general. If the completeness or accuracy of any item of information contained in a consumer's file at a consumer reporting agency is disputed by the consumer and the consumer notifies the agency directly of such dispute, the agency shall reinvestigate free of charge and record the current status of the disputed information, or delete the item from the file in accordance with paragraph (5), before the end of the 30-day period beginning on the date on which the agency receives the notice of the dispute from the consumer.

(B) Extension of period to reinvestigate. Except as provided in subparagraph (C), the 30-day period described in subparagraph (A) may be extended for not more than 15 additional days if the consumer reporting agency receives information from the consumer during that 30-day period that is relevant to the reinvestigation.

(C) Limitations on extension of period to reinvestigate. Subparagraph (B) shall not apply to any reinvestigation in which, during the 30-day period described in subparagraph (A), the information that is the subject of the reinvestigation is found to be inaccurate or incomplete or the consumer reporting agency determines that the information cannot be verified.

(2) Prompt notice of dispute to furnisher of information.

(A) In general. Before the expiration of the 5-business-day period beginning on the date on which a consumer reporting agency receives notice of a dispute from any consumer in accordance with paragraph (1), the agency shall provide notification of the dispute to any person who provided any item of information in dispute, at the address and in the manner established with the person. The notice shall include all relevant information regarding the dispute that the agency has received from the consumer.

(B) Provision of other information from consumer. The consumer reporting agency shall promptly provide to the person who provided the information in dispute all relevant information regarding the dispute that is received by the agency from the consumer after the period referred to in subparagraph (A) and before the end of the period referred to in paragraph (1)(A).

(3) Determination that dispute is frivolous or irrelevant.
(A) In general. Notwithstanding paragraph (1), a consumer reporting agency may terminate a reinvestigation of information disputed by a consumer under that paragraph if the agency reasonably determines that the dispute by the consumer is frivolous or irrelevant, including by reason of a failure by a consumer to provide sufficient information to investigate the disputed information.
(B) Notice of determination. Upon making any determination in accordance with subparagraph (A) that a dispute is frivolous or irrelevant, a consumer reporting agency shall notify the consumer of such determination not later than 5 business days after making such determination, by mail or, if authorized by the consumer for that purpose, by any other means available to the agency.
(C) Contents of notice. A notice under subparagraph (B) shall include
(i) the reasons for the determination under subparagraph (A); and
(ii) identification of any information required to investigate the disputed information, which may consist of a standardized form describing the general nature of such information.
(4) Consideration of consumer information. In conducting any reinvestigation under paragraph (1) with respect to disputed information in the file of any consumer, the consumer reporting agency shall review and consider all relevant information submitted by the consumer in the period described in paragraph (1)(A) with respect to such disputed information.
(5) Treatment of inaccurate or unverifiable information.
(A) In general. If, after any reinvestigation under paragraph (1) of any information disputed by a consumer, an item of the information is found to be inaccurate or incomplete or cannot be verified, the consumer reporting agency shall promptly delete that item of information from the consumer's file or modify that item of information, as appropriate, based on the results of the reinvestigation.
(B) Requirements relating to reinsertion of previously deleted material.
(i) Certification of accuracy of information. If any information is deleted from a consumer's file pursuant to subparagraph (A), the information may not be reinserted in the file by the consumer reporting agency unless the person who furnishes the information certifies that the information is complete and accurate.
(ii) Notice to consumer. If any information that has been deleted from a consumer's file pursuant to subparagraph (A) is reinserted in the file, the consumer reporting agency shall notify the consumer of the reinsertion in writing not later than 5 business days after the reinsertion or, if authorized by the consumer for that purpose, by any other means available to the agency.
(iii) Additional information. As part of, or in addition to, the notice under clause (ii), a consumer reporting agency shall provide to a consumer in writing not later than 5 business days after the date of the reinsertion
(I) a statement that the disputed information has been reinserted;
(II) the business name and address of any furnisher of information contacted and the telephone number of such furnisher, if reasonably available, or of any furnisher of information that contacted the consumer reporting agency, in connection with the reinsertion of such information; and
(III) a notice that the consumer has the right to add a statement to the consumer's file disputing the accuracy or completeness of the disputed information.
C) Procedures to prevent reappearance. A consumer reporting agency shall maintain reasonable procedures designed to

prevent the reappearance in a consumer's file, and in consumer reports on the consumer, of information that is deleted pursuant to this paragraph (other than information that is reinserted in accordance with subparagraph (B)(i)).
D) Automated reinvestigation system. Any consumer reporting agency that compiles and maintains files on consumers on a nationwide basis shall implement an automated system through which furnishers of information to that consumer reporting agency may report the results of a reinvestigation that finds incomplete or inaccurate information in a consumer's file to other such consumer reporting agencies.
(6) Notice of results of reinvestigation.
(A) In general. A consumer reporting agency shall provide written notice to a consumer of the results of a reinvestigation under this subsection not later than 5 business days after the completion of the reinvestigation, by mail or, if authorized by the consumer for that purpose, by other means available to the agency.
(B) Contents. As part of, or in addition to, the notice under subparagraph (A), a consumer reporting agency shall provide to a consumer in writing before the expiration of the 5-day period referred to in subparagraph (A)
(i) a statement that the reinvestigation is completed;
(ii) a consumer report that is based upon the consumer's file as that file is revised as a result of the reinvestigation;
(iii) a notice that, if requested by the consumer, a description of the procedure used to determine the accuracy and completeness of the information shall be provided to the consumer by the agency, including the business name and address of any furnisher of information contacted in connection with such information and the telephone number of such furnisher, if reasonably available;
(iv) a notice that the consumer has the right to add a statement to the consumer's file disputing the accuracy or completeness of the information; and
(v) a notice that the consumer has the right to request under subsection (d) that the consumer reporting agency furnish notifications under that subsection.
(7) Description of reinvestigation procedure. A consumer reporting agency shall provide to a consumer a description referred to in paragraph (6)(B)(iii) by not later than 15 days after receiving a request from the consumer for that description.
(8) Expedited dispute resolution. If a dispute regarding an item of information in a consumer's file at a consumer reporting agency is resolved in accordance with paragraph (5)(A) by the deletion of the disputed information by not later than 3 business days after the date on which the agency receives notice of the dispute from the consumer in accordance with paragraph (1)(A), then the agency shall not be required to comply with paragraphs (2), (6), and (7) with respect to that dispute if the agency
(A) provides prompt notice of the deletion to the consumer by telephone;
(B) includes in that notice, or in a written notice that accompanies a confirmation and consumer report provided in accordance with subparagraph (C), a statement of the consumer's right to request under subsection (d) that the agency furnish notifications under that subsection; and
(C) provides written confirmation of the deletion and a copy of a consumer report on the consumer that is based on the consumer's file after the deletion, not later than 5 business days after making the deletion.
(b) Statement of dispute. If the reinvestigation does not resolve the dispute, the consumer may file a brief statement setting forth the nature of the dispute. The consumer reporting agency may limit such statements to not more than one hundred words if it provides the consumer with assistance in writing a clear summary of the dispute.

(c) Notification of consumer dispute in subsequent consumer reports. Whenever a statement of a dispute is filed, unless there is reasonable grounds to believe that it is frivolous or irrelevant, the consumer reporting agency shall, in any subsequent consumer report containing the information in question, clearly note that it is disputed by the consumer and provide either the consumer's statement or a clear and accurate codification or summary thereof.

(d) Notification of deletion of disputed information. Following any deletion of information which is found to be inaccurate or whose accuracy can no longer be verified or any notation as to disputed information, the consumer reporting agency shall, at the request of the consumer, furnish notification that the item has been deleted or the statement, codification or summary pursuant to subsection (b) or (c) of this section to any person specifically designated by the consumer who has within two years prior thereto received a consumer report for employment purposes, or within six months prior thereto received a consumer report for any other purpose, which contained the deleted or disputed information.

§ 612. Charges for certain disclosures [15 U.S.C. § 1681j]

(a) Reasonable charges allowed for certain disclosures.

(1) In general. Except as provided in subsections (b), (c), and (d), a consumer reporting agency may impose a reasonable charge on a consumer

(A) for making a disclosure to the consumer pursuant to section 609 [§ 1681g], which charge

(i) shall not exceed $8;[3] and

(ii) shall be indicated to the consumer before making the disclosure; and

(B) for furnishing, pursuant to 611(d) [§ 1681i], following a reinvestigation under section 611(a) [§ 1681i], a statement, codification, or summary to a person designated by the consumer under that section after the 30-day period beginning on the date of notification of the consumer under paragraph (6) or (8) of section 611(a) [§ 1681i] with respect to the reinvestigation, which charge

(i) shall not exceed the charge that the agency would impose on each designated recipient for a consumer report; and

(ii) shall be indicated to the consumer before furnishing such information.

(2) Modification of amount. The Federal Trade Commission shall increase the amount referred to in paragraph (1)(A)(I) on January 1 of each year, based proportionally on changes in the Consumer Price Index, with fractional changes rounded to the nearest fifty cents.

(b) Free disclosure after adverse notice to consumer. Each consumer reporting agency that maintains a file on a consumer shall make all disclosures pursuant to section 609 [§ 1681g] without charge to the consumer if, not later than 60 days after receipt by such consumer of a notification pursuant to section 615 [§ 1681m], or of a notification from a debt collection agency affiliated with that consumer reporting agency stating that the consumer's credit rating may be or has been adversely affected, the consumer makes a request under section 609 [§ 1681g].

(c) Free disclosure under certain other circumstances. Upon the request of the consumer, a consumer reporting agency shall make all disclosures pursuant to section 609 [§ 1681g] once during any 12-month period without charge to that consumer if the consumer certifies in writing that the consumer

(1) is unemployed and intends to apply for employment in the 60-day period beginning on the date on which the certification is made;

(2) is a recipient of public welfare assistance; or

(3) has reason to believe that the file on the consumer at the agency contains inaccurate information due to fraud.

(d) Other charges prohibited. A consumer reporting agency shall not impose any charge on a consumer for providing any notification required by this title or making any disclosure required by this title, except as authorized by subsection (a).

§ 613. Public record information for employment purposes [15 U.S.C. § 1681j]

(a) In general. A consumer reporting agency which furnishes a consumer report for employment purposes and which for that purpose compiles and reports items of information on consumers which are matters of public record and are likely to have an adverse effect upon a consumer's ability to obtain employment shall

(1) at the time such public record information is reported to the user of such consumer report, notify the consumer of the fact that public record information is being reported by the consumer reporting agency, together with the name and address of the person to whom such information is being reported; or

(2) maintain strict procedures designed to insure that whenever public record information which is likely to have an adverse effect on a consumer's ability to obtain employment is reported it is complete and up to date. For purposes of this paragraph, items of public record relating to arrests, indictments, convictions, suits, tax liens, and outstanding judgments shall be considered up to date if the current public record status of the item at the time of the report is reported.

(b) Exemption for national security investigations. Subsection (a) does not apply in the case of an agency or department of the United States Government that seeks to obtain and use a consumer report for employment purposes, if the head of the agency or department makes a written finding as prescribed under section 604(b)(4)(A).

§ 614. Restrictions on investigative consumer reports [15 U.S.C. § 1681j]

Whenever a consumer reporting agency prepares an investigative consumer report, no adverse information in the consumer report (other than information which is a matter of public record) may be included in a subsequent consumer report unless such adverse information has been verified in the process of making such subsequent consumer report, or the adverse information was received within the three-month period preceding the date the subsequent report is furnished.

§ 615. Requirements on users of consumer reports [15 U.S.C. § 1681j]

(a) Duties of users taking adverse actions on the basis of information contained in consumer reports. If any person takes any adverse action with respect to any consumer that is based in whole or in part on any information contained in a consumer report, the person shall

(1) provide oral, written, or electronic notice of the adverse action to the consumer;

(2) provide to the consumer orally, in writing, or electronically

(A) the name, address, and telephone number of the consumer reporting agency (including a toll-free telephone number established by the agency if the agency compiles and maintains files on consumers on a nationwide basis) that furnished the report to the person; and

(B) a statement that the consumer reporting agency did not make the decision to take the adverse action and is unable to provide the consumer the specific reasons why the adverse action was taken; and

(3) provide to the consumer an oral, written, or electronic notice of the consumer's right

(A) to obtain, under section 612 [§ 1681j], a free copy of a consumer report on the consumer from the consumer reporting agency referred to in paragraph (2), which notice shall include an indication of the 60-day period under that section for obtaining such a copy; and

(B) to dispute, under section 611 [§ 1681i], with a consumer reporting agency the accuracy or completeness of any information in a consumer report furnished by the agency.

(b) Adverse action based on information obtained from third parties other than consumer reporting agencies.

(1) In general. Whenever credit for personal, family, or household purposes involving a consumer is denied or the charge for such credit is increased either wholly or partly because of information obtained from a person other than a consumer reporting agency bearing upon the consumer's credit worthiness, credit standing, credit capacity, character, general reputation, personal characteristics, or mode of living, the user of such information shall, within a reasonable period of time, upon the consumer's written request for the reasons for such adverse action received within sixty days after learning of such adverse action, disclose the nature of the information to the consumer. The user of such information shall clearly and accurately disclose to the consumer his right to make such written request at the time such adverse action is communicated to the consumer.

(2) Duties of person taking certain actions based on information provided by affiliate.

(A) Duties, generally. If a person takes an action described in subparagraph (B) with respect to a consumer, based in whole or in part on information described in subparagraph (C), the person shall

(i) notify the consumer of the action, including a statement that the consumer may obtain the information in accordance with clause (ii); and

(ii) upon a written request from the consumer received within 60 days after transmittal of the notice required by clause (I), disclose to the consumer the nature of the information upon which the action is based by not later than 30 days after receipt of the request.

(B) Action described. An action referred to in subparagraph (A) is an adverse action described in section 603(k)(1)(A) [§ 1681a], taken in connection with a transaction initiated by the consumer, or any adverse action described in clause (i) or (ii) of section 603(k)(1)(B) [§ 1681a].

(C) Information described. Information referred to in subparagraph (A)

(i) except as provided in clause (ii), is information that

(I) is furnished to the person taking the action by a person related by common ownership or affiliated by common corporate control to the person taking the action; and

(II) bears on the credit worthiness, credit standing, credit capacity, character, general reputation, personal characteristics, or mode of living of the consumer; and

(ii) does not include

(I) information solely as to transactions or experiences between the consumer and the person furnishing the information; or

(II) information in a consumer report.

(c) Reasonable procedures to assure compliance. No person shall be held liable for any violation of this section if he shows by a preponderance of the evidence that at the time of the alleged violation he maintained reasonable procedures to assure compliance with the provisions of this section.

(d) Duties of users making written credit or insurance solicitations on the basis of information contained in consumer files.

(1) In general. Any person who uses a consumer report on any consumer in connection with any credit or insurance transaction that is not initiated by the consumer, that is provided to that person under section 604(c)(1)(B) [§ 1681b], shall provide with each written solicitation made to the consumer regarding the transaction a clear and conspicuous statement that

(A) information contained in the consumer's consumer report was used in connection with the transaction;
(B) the consumer received the offer of credit or insurance because the consumer satisfied the criteria for credit worthiness or insurability under which the consumer was selected for the offer;
(C) if applicable, the credit or insurance may not be extended if, after the consumer responds to the offer, the consumer does not meet the criteria used to select the consumer for the offer or any applicable criteria bearing on credit worthiness or insurability or does not furnish any required collateral;
(D) the consumer has a right to prohibit information contained in the consumer's file with any consumer reporting agency from being used in connection with any credit or insurance transaction that is not initiated by the consumer; and
(E) the consumer may exercise the right referred to in subparagraph (D) by notifying a notification system established under section 604(e) [§ 1681b].
(2) Disclosure of address and telephone number. A statement under paragraph (1) shall include the address and toll-free telephone number of the appropriate notification system established under section 604(e) [§ 1681b].
(3) Maintaining criteria on file. A person who makes an offer of credit or insurance to a consumer under a credit or insurance transaction described in paragraph (1) shall maintain on file the criteria used to select the consumer to receive the offer, all criteria bearing on credit worthiness or insurability, as applicable, that are the basis for determining whether or not to extend credit or insurance pursuant to the offer, and any requirement for the furnishing of collateral as a condition of the extension of credit or insurance, until the expiration of the 3-year period beginning on the date on which the offer is made to the consumer.
(4) Authority of federal agencies regarding unfair or deceptive acts or practices not affected. This section is not intended to affect the authority of any Federal or State agency to enforce a prohibition against unfair or deceptive acts or practices, including the making of false or misleading statements in connection with a credit or insurance transaction that is not initiated by the consumer.
§ 616. Civil liability for willful noncompliance [15 U.S.C. § 1681j]
(a) In general. Any person who willfully fails to comply with any requirement imposed under this title with respect to any consumer is liable to that consumer in an amount equal to the sum of
(1)(A) any actual damages sustained by the consumer as a result of the failure or damages of not less than $100 and not more than $1,000; or
(B) in the case of liability of a natural person for obtaining a consumer report under false pretenses or knowingly without a permissible purpose, actual damages sustained by the consumer as a result of the failure or $1,000, whichever is greater;
(2) such amount of punitive damages as the court may allow; and
(3) in the case of any successful action to enforce any liability under this section, the costs of the action together with reasonable attorney's fees as determined by the court.
(b) Civil liability for knowing noncompliance. Any person who obtains a consumer report from a consumer reporting agency under false pretenses or knowingly without a permissible purpose shall be liable to the consumer reporting agency for actual damages sustained by the consumer reporting agency or $1,000, whichever is greater.
(c) Attorney's fees. Upon a finding by the court that an unsuccessful pleading, motion, or other paper filed in connection with an action under this section was filed in bad faith or for purposes of harassment, the court shall

award to the prevailing party attorney's fees reasonable in relation to the work expended in responding to the pleading, motion, or other paper.

§ 617. Civil liability for negligent noncompliance[15 U.S.C. § 1681j]

(a) In general. Any person who is negligent in fai ling to comply with any requirement imposed under this title with respect to any consumer is liable to that consumer in an amount equal to the sum of

(1) any actual damages sustained by the consumer as a result of the failure;

(2) in the case of any successful action to enforce any liability under this section, the costs of the action together with reasonable attorney's fees as determined by the court.

(b) Attorney's fees. On a finding by the court that an unsuccessful pleading, motion, or other paper filed in connection with an action under this section was filed in bad faith or for purposes of harassment, the court shall award to the prevailing party attorney's fees reasonable in relation to the work expended in responding to the pleading, motion, or other paper.

§ 618. Jurisdiction of courts; limitation of actions [15 U.S.C. § 1681j]

An action to enforce any liability created under this title may be brought in any appropriate United States district court without regard to the amount in controversy, or in any other court of competent jurisdiction, within two years from the date on which the liability arises, except that where a defendant has materially and willfully misrepresented any information required under this title to be disclosed to an individual and the information so misrepresented is material to the establishment of the defendant's liability to that individual under this title, the action may be brought at any time within two years after discovery by the individual of the misrepresentation.

§ 619. Obtaining information under false pretenses [15 U.S.C. § 1681j]

Any person who knowingly and willfully obtains information on a consumer from a consumer reporting agency under false pretenses shall be fined under title 18, United States Code, imprisoned for not more than 2 years, or both.

§ 620. Unauthorized disclosures by officers or employees [15 U.S.C. § 1681j]

Any officer or employee of a consumer reporting agency who knowingly and willfully provides information concerning an individual from the agency's files to a person not authorized to receive that information shall be fined under title 18, United States Code, imprisoned for not more than 2 years, or both.

§ 621. Administrative enforcement [15 U.S.C. § 1681j]

(a) (1) Enforcement by Federal Trade Commission. Compliance with the requirements imposed under this title shall be enforced under the Federal Trade Commission Act [15 U.S.C. §§ 41 et seq.] by the Federal Trade Commission with respect to consumer reporting agencies and all other persons subject thereto, except to the extent that enforcement of the requirements imposed under this title is specifically committed to some other government agency under subsection (b) hereof. For the purpose of the exercise by the Federal Trade Commission of its functions and powers under the Federal Trade Commission Act, a violation of any requirement or prohibition imposed under this title shall constitute an unfair or deceptive act or practice in commerce in violation of section 5(a) of the Federal Trade Commission Act [15 U.S.C. § 45(a)] and shall be subject to enforcement by the Federal Trade Commission under section 5(b) thereof [15 U.S.C. § 45(b)] with respect to any consumer reporting agency or person subject to enforcement by the Federal Trade Commission pursuant to this subsection, irrespective of whether that person is engaged in commerce or meets any other jurisdictional tests in the Federal Trade Commission Act. The Federal Trade Commission shall have such procedural, investigative, and enforcement powers, including the power to issue procedural rules in enforcing compliance with the requirements imposed under this title and to require the filing of reports, the production of documents, and the appearance of witnesses as though the applicable terms and conditions of the Federal Trade Commission Act were part of this title. Any person violating any of the provisions of this title shall be subject to the penalties and entitled to the privileges and immunities provided in the Federal Trade Commission Act as though the applicable terms and provisions thereof were part of this title.

(2)(A) In the event of a knowing violation, which constitutes a pattern or practice of violations of this title, the Commission may commence a civil action to recover a civil penalty in a district court of the United States against any person that violates this title. In such action, such person shall be liable for a civil penalty of not more than $2,500 per violation.

(B) In determining the amount of a civil penalty under subparagraph (A), the court shall take into account the degree of culpability, any history of prior such conduct, ability to pay, effect on ability to continue to do business, and such other matters as justice may require.

(3) Notwithstanding paragraph (2), a court may not impose any civil penalty on a person for a violation of section 623(a)(1) [§ 1681s-2] unless the person has been enjoined from committing the violation, or ordered not to commit the violation, in an action or proceeding brought by or on behalf of the Federal Trade Commission, and has violated the injunction or order, and the court may not impose any civil penalty for any violation occurring before the date of the violation of the injunction or order.

(b) Enforcement by other agencies. Compliance with the requirements imposed under this title with respect to consumer reporting agencies, persons who use consumer reports from such agencies, persons who furnish information to such agencies, and users of information that are subject to subsection (d) of section 615 [§ 1681m] shall be enforced under

(1) section 8 of the Federal Deposit Insurance Act [12 U.S.C. § 1818], in the case of

(A) national banks, and Federal branches and Federal agencies of foreign banks, by the Office of the Comptroller of the Currency;

(B) member banks of the Federal Reserve System (other than national banks), branches and agencies of foreign banks (other than Federal branches, Federal agencies, and insured State branches of foreign banks), commercial lending companies owned or controlled by foreign banks, and organizations operating under section 25 or 25(a) [25A] of the Federal Reserve Act [12 U.S.C. §§ 601 et seq., §§ 611 et seq], by the Board of Governors of the Federal Reserve System; and

(C) banks insured by the Federal Deposit Insurance Corporation (other than members of the Federal Reserve System) and insured State branches of foreign banks, by the Board of Directors of the Federal Deposit Insurance Corporation;

(2) section 8 of the Federal Deposit Insurance Act [12 U.S.C. § 1818], by the Director of the Office of Thrift Supervision, in the case of a savings association the deposits of which are insured by the Federal Deposit Insurance Corporation;

(3) the Federal Credit Union Act [12 U.S.C. §§ 1751 et seq.], by the Administrator of the National Credit Union Administration [National Credit Union Administration Board] with respect to any Federal credit union;

(4) subtitle IV of title 49 [49 U.S.C. §§ 10101 et seq.], by the Secretary of Transportation, with respect to all carriers

subject to the jurisdiction of the Surface Transportation Board;
(5) the Federal Aviation Act of 1958 [49 U.S.C. Appx §§ 1301 et seq.], by the Secretary of Transportation with respect to any air carrier or foreign air carrier subject to that Act [49 U.S.C. Appx §§ 1301 et seq.]; and
(6) the Packers and Stockyards Act, 1921 [7 U.S.C. §§ 181 et seq.] (except as provided in section 406 of that Act [7 U.S.C. §§ 226 and 227]), by the Secretary of Agriculture with respect to any activities subject to that Act.
The terms used in paragraph (1) that are not defined in this title or otherwise defined in section 3(s) of the Federal Deposit Insurance Act (12 U.S.C. §1813(s)) shall have the meaning given to them in section 1(b) of the International Banking Act of 1978 (12 U.S.C. § 3101).
(c) State action for violations.
(1) Authority of states. In addition to such other remedies as are provided under State law, if the chief law enforcement officer of a State, or an official or agency designated by a State, has reason to believe that any person has violated or is violating this title, the State
(A) may bring an action to enjoin such violation in any appropriate United States district court or in any other court of competent jurisdiction;
(B) subject to paragraph (5), may bring an action on behalf of the residents of the State to recover
(i) damages for which the person is liable to such residents under sections 616 and 617 [§§ 1681n and 1681o] as a result of the violation;
(ii) in the case of a violation of section 623(a) [§ 1681s-2], damages for which the person would, but for section 623(c) [§ 1681s-2], be liable to such residents as a result of the violation; or
(iii) damages of not more than $1,000 for each willful or negligent violation; and

(C) in the case of any successful action under subparagraph (A) or (B), shall be awarded the costs of the action and reasonable attorney fees as determined by the court.
(2) Rights of federal regulators. The State shall serve prior written notice of any action under paragraph (1) upon the Federal Trade Commission or the appropriate Federal regulator determined under subsection (b) and provide the Commission or appropriate Federal regulator with a copy of its complaint, except in any case in which such prior notice is not feasible, in which case the State shall serve such notice immediately upon instituting such action. The Federal Trade Commission or appropriate Federal regulator shall have the right
(A) to intervene in the action;
(B) upon so intervening, to be heard on all matters arising therein;
(C) to remove the action to the appropriate United States district court; and
(D) to file petitions for appeal.
(3) Investigatory powers. For purposes of bringing any action under this subsection, nothing in this subsection shall prevent the chief law enforcement officer, or an official or agency designated by a State, from exercising the powers conferred on the chief law enforcement officer or such official by the laws of such State to conduct investigations or to administer oaths or affirmations or to compel the attendance of witnesses or the production of documentary and other evidence.
(4) Limitation on state action while federal action pending. If the Federal Trade Commission or the appropriate Federal regulator has instituted a civil action or an administrative action under section 8 of the Federal Deposit Insurance Act for a violation of this title, no State may, during the pendency of such action, bring an action under this section against

any defendant named in the complaint of the Commission or the appropriate Federal regulator for any violation of this title that is alleged in that complaint.

(5) Limitations on state actions for violation of section 623(a)(1) [§ 1681s-2].

(A) Violation of injunction required. A State may not bring an action against a person under paragraph (1)(B) for a violation of section 623(a)(1) [§ 1681s-2], unless

(i) the person has been enjoined from committing the violation, in an action brought by the State under paragraph (1)(A); and

(ii) the person has violated the injunction.

(B) Limitation on damages recoverable. In an action against a person under paragraph (1)(B) for a violation of section 623(a)(1) [§ 1681s-2], a State may not recover any damages incurred before the date of the violation of an injunction on which the action is based.

(d) Enforcement under other authority. For the purpose of the exercise by any agency referred to in subsection (b) of this section of its powers under any Act referred to in that subsection, a violation of any requirement imposed under this title shall be deemed to be a violation of a requirement imposed under that Act. In addition to its powers under any provision of law specifically referred to in subsection (b) of this section, each of the agencies referred to in that subsection may exercise, for the purpose of enforcing compliance with any requirement imposed under this title any other authority conferred on it by law.

(e) Regulatory authority

(1) The Federal banking agencies referred to in paragraphs (1) and (2) of subsection (b) shall jointly prescribe such regulations as necessary to carry out the purposes of this Act with respect to any persons identified under paragraphs (1) and (2) of subsection (b), and the Board of Governors of the Federal Reserve System shall have authority to prescribe regulations consistent with such joint regulations with respect to bank holding companies and affiliates (other than depository institutions and consumer reporting agencies) of such holding companies.

(2) The Board of the National Credit Union Administration shall prescribe such regulations as necessary to carry out the purposes of this Act with respect to any persons identified under paragraph (3) of subsection (b).

§ 622. Information on overdue child support obligations [15 U.S.C. § 1681j]

Notwithstanding any other provision of this title, a consumer reporting agency shall include in any consumer report furnished by the agency in accordance with section 604 [§ 1681b] of this title, any information on the failure of the consumer to pay overdue support which

(1) is provided

(A) to the consumer reporting agency by a State or local child support enforcement agency; or

(B) to the consumer reporting agency and verified by any local, State, or Federal government agency; and

(2) antedates the report by 7 years or less.

§ 623. Responsibilities of furnishers of information to consumer reporting agencies [15 U.S.C. § 1681s-2]

(a) Duty of furnishers of information to provide accurate information.

(1) Prohibition.

(A) Reporting information with actual knowledge of errors. A person shall not furnish any information relating to a consumer to any consumer reporting agency if the person knows or consciously avoids knowing that the information is inaccurate.

(B) Reporting information after notice and confirmation of errors. A person shall not furnish information relating to a consumer to any consumer reporting agency if

(i) the person has been notified by the consumer, at the address specified by the person for such notices, that specific information is inaccurate; and

(ii) the information is, in fact, inaccurate.

(C) No address requirement. A person who clearly and conspicuously specifies to the consumer an address for notices referred to in subparagraph (B) shall not be subject to subparagraph (A); however, nothing in subparagraph (B) shall require a person to specify such an address.

(2) Duty to correct and update information. A person who

(A) regularly and in the ordinary course of business furnishes information to one or more consumer reporting agencies about the person's transactions or experiences with any consumer; and

(B) has furnished to a consumer reporting agency information that the person determines is not complete or accurate, shall promptly notify the consumer reporting agency of that determination and provide to the agency any corrections to that information, or any additional information, that is necessary to make the information provided by the person to the agency complete and accurate, and shall not thereafter furnish to the agency any of the information that remains not complete or accurate.

(3) Duty to provide notice of dispute. If the completeness or accuracy of any information furnished by any person to any consumer reporting agency is disputed to such person by a consumer, the person may not furnish the information to any consumer reporting agency without notice that such information is disputed by the consumer.

(4) Duty to provide notice of closed accounts. A person who regularly and in the ordinary course of business furnishes information to a consumer reporting agency regarding a consumer who has a credit account with that person shall notify the agency of the voluntary closure of the account by the consumer, in information regularly furnished for the period in which the account is closed.

(5) Duty to provide notice of delinquency of accounts. A person who furnishes information to a consumer reporting agency regarding a delinquent account being placed for collection, charged to profit or loss, or subjected to any similar action shall, not later than 90 days after furnishing the information, notify the agency of the month and year of the commencement of the delinquency that immediately preceded the action.

(b) Duties of furnishers of information upon notice of dispute.

(1) In general. After receiving notice pursuant to section 611(a)(2) [§ 1681i] of a dispute with regard to the completeness or accuracy of any information provided by a person to a consumer reporting agency, the person shall

(A) conduct an investigation with respect to the disputed information;

(B) review all relevant information provided by the consumer reporting agency pursuant to section 611(a)(2) [§ 1681i];

(C) report the results of the investigation to the consumer reporting agency; and

(D) if the investigation finds that the information is incomplete or inaccurate, report those results to all other consumer reporting agencies to which the person furnished the information and that compile and maintain files on consumers on a nationwide basis.

(2) Deadline. A person shall complete all investigations, reviews, and reports required under paragraph (1) regarding information provided by the person to a consumer reporting agency, before the expiration of the period under section 611(a)(1) [§ 1681i] within which the consumer reporting agency is required to complete actions required by that section regarding that information.

(c) Limitation on liability. Sections 616 and 617 [§§ 1681n and 1681o] do not apply to any failure to comply with subsection (a), except as provided in section 621(c)(1)(B) [§ 1681s].
(d) Limitation on enforcement. Subsection (a) shall be enforced exclusively under section 621 [§ 1681s] by the Federal agencies and officials and the State officials identified in that section.
§ 624. Relation to State laws [15 U.S.C. § 1681t]
(a) In general. Except as provided in subsections (b) and (c), this title does not annul, alter, affect, or exempt any person subject to the provisions of this title from complying with the laws of any State with respect to the collection, distribution, or use of any information on consumers, except to the extent that those laws are inconsistent with any provision of this title, and then only to the extent of the inconsistency.
(b) General exceptions. No requirement or prohibition may be imposed under the laws of any State
(1) with respect to any subject matter regulated under
(A) subsection (c) or (e) of section 604 [§ 1681b], relating to the prescreening of consumer reports;
(B) section 611 [§ 1681i], relating to the time by which a consumer reporting agency must take any action, including the provision of notification to a consumer or other person, in any procedure related to the disputed accuracy of information in a consumer's file, except that this subparagraph shall not apply to any State law in effect on the date of enactment of the Consumer Credit Reporting Reform Act of 1996;
(C) subsections (a) and (b) of section 615 [§ 1681m], relating to the duties of a person who takes any adverse action with respect to a consumer;
(D) section 615(d) [§ 1681m], relating to the duties of persons who use a consumer report of a consumer in connection with any credit or insurance transaction that is not initiated by the consumer and that consists of a firm offer of credit or insurance;
(E) section 605 [§ 1681c], relating to information contained in consumer reports, except that this subparagraph shall not apply to any State law in effect on the date of enactment of the Consumer Credit Reporting Reform Act of 1996; or
(F) section 623 [§ 1681s-2], relating to the responsibilities of persons who furnish information to consumer reporting agencies, except that this paragraph shall not apply
(i) with respect to section 54A(a) of chapter 93 of the Massachusetts Annotated Laws (as in effect on the date of enactment of the Consumer Credit Reporting Reform Act of 1996); or
(ii) with respect to section 1785.25(a) of the California Civil Code (as in effect on the date of enactment of the Consumer Credit Reporting Reform Act of 1996);
(2) with respect to the exchange of information among persons affiliated by common ownership or common corporate control, except that this paragraph shall not apply with respect to subsection (a) or (c)(1) of section 2480e of title 9, Vermont Statutes Annotated (as in effect on the date of enactment of the Consumer Credit Reporting Reform Act of 1996); or
(3) with respect to the form and content of any disclosure required to be made under section 609(c) [§ 1681g].
(c) Definition of firm offer of credit or insurance. Notwithstanding any definition of the term "firm offer of credit or insurance" (or any equivalent term) under the laws of any State, the definition of that term contained in section 603(*l*) [§ 1681a] shall be construed to apply in the enforcement and interpretation of the laws of any State governing consumer reports.
(d) Limitations. Subsections (b) and (c)

(1) do not affect any settlement, agreement, or consent judgment between any State Attorney General and any consumer reporting agency in effect on the date of enactment of the Consumer Credit Reporting Reform Act of 1996; and

(2) do not apply to any provision of State law (including any provision of a State constitution) that

(A) is enacted after January 1, 2004;

(B) states explicitly that the provision is intended to supplement this title; and

(C) gives greater protection to consumers than is provided under this title.

§ 625. Disclosures to FBI for counterintelligence purposes [15 U.S.C. § 1681u]

(a) Identity of financial institutions. Notwithstanding section 604 [§ 1681b] or any other provision of this title, a consumer reporting agency shall furnish to the Federal Bureau of Investigation the names and addresses of all financial institutions (as that term is defined in section 1101 of the Right to Financial Privacy Act of 1978 [12 U.S.C. § 3401]) at which a consumer maintains or has maintained an account, to the extent that information is in the files of the agency, when presented with a written request for that information, signed by the Director of the Federal Bureau of Investigation, or the Director's designee in a position not lower than Deputy Assistant Director at Bureau headquarters or a Special Agent in Charge of a Bureau field office designated by the Director, which certifies compliance with this section. The Director or the Director's designee may make such a certification only if the Director or the Director's designee has determined in writing, that such information is sought for the conduct of an authorized investigation to protect against international terrorism or clandestine intelligence activities, provided that such an investigation of a United States person is not conducted solely upon the basis of activities protected by the first amendment to the Constitution of the United States.

(b) Identifying information. Notwithstanding the provisions of section 604 [§ 1681b] or any other provision of this title, a consumer reporting agency shall furnish identifying information respecting a consumer, limited to name, address, former addresses, places of employment, or former places of employment, to the Federal Bureau of Investigation when presented with a written request, signed by the Director or the Director's designee, which certifies compliance with this subsection. The Director or the Director's designee in a position not lower than Deputy Assistant Director at Bureau headquarters or a Special Agent in Charge of a Bureau field office designated by the Director may make such a certification only if the Director or the Director's designee has determined in writing that such information is sought for the conduct of an authorized investigation to protect against international terrorism or clandestine intelligence activities, provided that such an investigation of a United States person is not conducted solely upon the basis of activities protected by the first amendment to the Constitution of the United States.

(c) Court order for disclosure of consumer reports. Notwithstanding section 604 [§ 1681b] or any other provision of this title, if requested in writing by the Director of the Federal Bureau of Investigation, or a designee of the Director in a position not lower than Deputy Assistant Director at Bureau headquarters or a Special Agent in Charge of a Bureau field office designated by the Director, a court may issue an order ex parte directing a consumer reporting agency to furnish a consumer report to the Federal Bureau of Investigation, upon a showing in camera that the consumer report is sought for the conduct of an authorized investigation to protect against international terrorism or clandestine intelligence activities, provided that such an investigation of a United States person is not conducted solely upon the basis of activities protected by the first amendment to the Constitution of the United States.

The terms of an order issued under this subsection shall not disclose that the order is issued for purposes of a counterintelligence investigation.

(d) Confidentiality. No consumer reporting agency or officer, employee, or agent of a consumer reporting agency shall disclose to any person, other than those officers, employees, or agents of a consumer reporting agency necessary to fulfill the requirement to disclose information to the Federal Bureau of Investigation under this section, that the Federal Bureau of Investigation has sought or obtained the identity of financial institutions or a consumer report respecting any consumer under subsection (a), (b), or (c), and no consumer reporting agency or officer, employee, or agent of a consumer reporting agency shall include in any consumer report any information that would indicate that the Federal Bureau of Investigation has sought or obtained such information or a consumer report.
(e) Payment of fees. The Federal Bureau of Investigation shall, subject to the availability of appropriations, pay to the consumer reporting agency assembling or providing report or information in accordance with procedures established under this section a fee for reimbursement for such costs as are reasonably necessary and which have been directly incurred in searching, reproducing, or transporting books, papers, records, or other data required or requested to be produced under this section.
(f) Limit on dissemination. The Federal Bureau of Investigation may not disseminate information obtained pursuant to this section outside of the Federal Bureau of Investigation, except to other Federal agencies as may be necessary for the approval or conduct of a foreign counterintelligence investigation, or, where the information concerns a person subject to the Uniform Code of Military Justice, to appropriate investigative authorities within the military department concerned as may be necessary for the conduct of a joint foreign counterintelligence investigation.
(g) Rules of construction. Nothing in this section shall be construed to prohibit information from being furnished by the Federal Bureau of Investigation pursuant to a subpoena or court order, in connection with a judicial or administrative proceeding to enforce the provisions of this Act. Nothing in this section shall be construed to authorize or permit the withholding of information from the Congress.
(h) Reports to Congress. On a semiannual basis, the Attorney General shall fully inform the Permanent Select Committee on Intelligence and the Committee on Banking, Finance and Urban Affairs of the House of Representatives, and the Select Committee on Intelligence and the Committee on Banking, Housing, and Urban Affairs of the Senate concerning all requests made pursuant to subsections (a), (b), and (c).
(i) Damages. Any agency or department of the United States obtaining or disclosing any consumer reports, records, or information contained therein in violation of this section is liable to the consumer to whom such consumer reports, records, or information relate in an amount equal to the sum of
(1) $100, without regard to the volume of consumer reports, records, or information involved;
(2) any actual damages sustained by the consumer as a result of the disclosure;
(3) if the violation is found to have been willful or intentional, such punitive damages as a court may allow; and
(4) in the case of any successful action to enforce liability under this subsection, the costs of the action, together with reasonable attorney fees, as determined by the court.
(j) Disciplinary actions for violations. If a court determines that any agency or department of the United States has violated any provision of this section and the court finds that the circumstances surrounding the violation raise questions of whether or not an officer or employee of the agency or department acted willfully or intentionally with respect to the violation, the agency or department shall promptly initiate a proceeding to determine whether or not disciplinary action is warranted against the officer or employee who was responsible for the violation.
(k) Good-faith exception. Notwithstanding any other provision of this title, any consumer reporting agency or agent

or employee thereof making disclosure of consumer reports or identifying information pursuant to this subsection in good-faith reliance upon a certification of the Federal Bureau of Investigation pursuant to provisions of this section shall not be liable to any person for such disclosure under this title, the constitution of any State, or any law or regulation of any State or any political subdivision of any State.

(l) Limitation of remedies. Notwithstanding any other provision of this title, the remedies and sanctions set forth in this section shall be the only judicial remedies and sanctions for violation of this section.

(m) Injunctive relief. In addition to any other remedy contained in this section, injunctive relief shall be available to require compliance with the procedures of this section. In the event of any successful action under this subsection, costs together with reasonable attorney fees, as determined by the court, may be recovered.

§ 626. Disclosures to governmental agencies for counterterrorism purposes [15 U.S.C. §1681v]

(a) Disclosure. Notwithstanding section 604 or any other provision of this title, a consumer reporting agency shall furnish a consumer report of a consumer and all other information in a consumer's file to a government agency authorized to conduct investigations of, or intelligence or counterintelligence activities or analysis related to, international terrorism when presented with a written certification by such government agency that such information is necessary for the agency's conduct or such investigation, activity or analysis.

(b) Form of certification. The certification described in subsection (a) shall be signed by a supervisory official designated by the head of a Federal agency or an officer of a Federal agency whose appointment to office is required to be made by the President, by and with the advice and consent of the Senate.

(c) Confidentiality. No consumer reporting agency, or officer, employee, or agent of such consumer reporting agency, shall disclose to any person, or specify in any consumer report, that a government agency has sought or obtained access to information under subsection (a).

(d) Rule of construction. Nothing in section 625 shall be construed to limit the authority of the Director of the Federal Bureau of Investigation under this section.

(e) Safe harbor. Notwithstanding any other provision of this title, any consumer reporting agency or agent or employee thereof making disclosure of consumer reports or other information pursuant to this section in good-faith reliance upon a certification of a governmental agency pursuant to the provisions of this section shall not be liable to any person for such disclosure under this subchapter, the constitution of any State, or any law or regulation of any State or any political subdivision of any State.

Legislative History

House Reports:

No. 91-975 (Comm. on Banking and Currency) and

No. 91-1587 (Comm. of Conference)

Senate Reports:

No. 91-1139 accompanying S. 3678 (Comm. on Banking and Currency)

Congressional Record, Vol. 116 (1970)

May 25, considered and passed House.

Sept. 18, considered and passed Senate, amended.

Oct. 9, Senate agreed to conference report.

Oct. 13, House agreed to conference report.

Enactment:

Public Law No. 91-508 (October 26, 1970):

Amendments: Public Law Nos.

95-473 (October 17, 1978)

95-598 (November 6, 1978)

98-443 (October 4, 1984)

101-73 (August 9, 1989)

102-242 (December 19, 1991)

102-537 (October 27, 1992)

102-550 (October 28, 1992)

103-325 (September 23, 1994)

104-88 (December 29, 1995)

104-93 (January 6, 1996)

104-193 (August 22, 1996)

104-208 (September 30, 1996)

105-107 (November 20, 1997)

105-347 (November 2, 1998)

106-102 (November 12, 1999)

107-56 (October 26, 2001)

Endnotes:

1. The reporting periods have been lengthened for certain adverse information pertaining to U.S. Government insured or guaranteed student loans, or pertaining to national direct student loans. See sections 430A(f) and 463(c)(3) of the Higher Education Act of 1965, 20 U.S.C. 1080a(f) and 20 U.S.C. 1087cc(c)(3), respectively.

2. Should read "paragraphs (4) and (5)...." Prior Section 605(a)(6) was amended and re-designated as Section 605(a)(5) in November 1998.

3. The Federal Trade Commission increased the maximum allowable charge to $9.00, effective January 1, 2002. 66 Fed. Reg. 63545 (Dec. 7, 2001).

ECONOMIC EMPOWERMENT RESOURCES

REQUIRED RESOURCES

Everything You Wanted To Know About Developing Your Life's Purpose Plan and Reaching Your Goals (Coming Soon!!!).
Author(s): Renee D. Crenshaw and Anthony B. Miles
Description: In this 90 min Audio Compact Disk, Personal Finance Experts Renee D. Crenshaw and Anthony B. Miles provide tools, tips and hidden secrets to developing your life's purpose plan and reaching your financial goals.
To reserve your copy: call (215) 222-0390

One Minute Millionaire -The Enlightened Way To Wealth
Author(s): Mark Victor Hansen and Robert Allen
Description: One Minute Millionaire: Robert Allen and Mark Hansen from the enlightened millionaire institute teach you how to become a millionaire one minute at a time by utilizing their proven coaching program and secret methods.
Available: www.amazon.com

Cashflow Quadrant - Rich Dad's Guide to Financial Freedom
Author(s): Robert T. Kiyosaki with Sharon Lechter
Description: If your assets generate cash flow for you, then you don't need to work as hard. Plain and simple. By understanding each of the four quadrants that identify you in your business career, you'll more clearly see the path that is right for you to achieve financial freedom.
Available: www.amazon.com

CREDIT

Everything You Wanted To Know About Credit But Were Too Ashamed To Ask
Tools, Tips and Hidden Secrets to Fixing Bad Credit, Building and Maintaining AAA Credit
Author(s): Renee D. Crenshaw and Anthony B. Miles
Description: In this 192-page credit resource guide, Personal Finance Experts Renee D. Crenshaw and Anthony B. Miles provide tools, tips and hidden secrets to fixing bad credit, building and maintaining AAA credit.
Available: www.atlasbooks.com or 1-800-booklog

DEBT ELIMINATION

Transform Debt to Wealth
Author(s): John Cummuttu
Description: This program teaches how-to Get Completely Out Of Debt (including your home mortgage) and start building real wealth in five to seven years!
Available: www.amazon.com

HOMEOWNERSHIP

Everything You Wanted To Know About Homeownership
Author(s): Landus Nelson and David Nelson (Coming Soon!!!)
Description: In this 220-page homeownership resource guide, Homeownership Experts Landus and David Nelson provide tools, tips and hidden secrets to buying, maintaining and selling a home.
To reserve your copy: call (215) 222-0390

MONEY & KIDS

Rich Dad's Rich Kid Smart Kid - Giving your Children a Financial Headstart
Author(s): Robert T. Kiyosaki, Sharon L. Lechter
Description: Give your child a financial head start by awakening your child's love of learning to be financially free. Imagine the affect you can have on their lives when they start early. Rich Dad's Rich Kid Smart Kid is designed to help you give your child the same inspiring and practical financial knowledge that Robert Kiyosaki's rich dad gave him.
Available: www.amazon.com

Cash Flow for Kids Board Game - Giving your Children a Financial Headstart
Author(s): Robert T. Kiyosaki, Sharon L. Lechter
Description: Give your children the financial head start necessary to thrive in today's fast paced and changing world. Schools teach children how to work for money. CASHFLOW™ for Kids teaches children how to have money work for them. CASHFLOW™ for Kids is a complete educational package which includes the book and audiocassette titled "Rich Dad's Guide to Raising Your Child's Financial I.Q." CASHFLOW™ for Kids is recommended for children ages 6 and older.
Available: www.amazon.com

CREATING MULTIPLE STREAMS OF INCOME

Speak and Grow Rich
Author(s): Dottie Walters, Lilly Walters
Description: Here are all the techniques and shortcuts today's top speakers use to generate annual fees of up to $800,000 and more! Now you can use these techniques to generate the same kind of income for yourself through a career in paid, professional speaking.
Available: www.amazon.com

Cash Flow 101 Board Game
Author(s): Robert T. Kiyosaki, Sharon L. Lechter
Description: CASHFLOW® 101 is an educational program that teaches accounting, finance, and investing at the same time and makes learning fun.
Available: www.amazon.com

SELF-PUBLISHING

The Self-Publishing Manual
Author(s): *Dan Poynter*
Description: How-to write, print and sell your own books
Available: www.amazon.com

Literary Law Guide for Authors
Author(s): *Tonya Marie Evans and Susan Borden Evans*
Description: Copyright, Trademarks, Contracts and Plain Language
Available: www.amazon.com

BUSINESS OWNERSHIP

Protecting Your #1 Asset - Creating Fortunes from Your Ideas
Author(s): Michael Lechter Esq.
Description: Learn how to turn ideas into assets. This intellectual property handbook guides you from protection to creating cash flow.
Available: www.amazon.com

Own Your Own Corporation - Why the Rich Own Their Own Companies and Everyone Else Works for Them
Author(s): *Garrett Sutton Esq.*
Description: Learn the advantages and principles of setting up corporations - to run your business, protect your assets, and lower your taxes.
Available: www.amazon.com

Sales Dogs - Improving Your #1 Business Skill
Author(s): *Blair Singer*
Description: You don't have to be an attack dog to be successful in sales. Learn how to reduce your sales "effort", and increase your sales "results". Blair Singer Sales Communication Specialist
Available: www.amazon.com

REAL ESTATE INVESTING

Everything You Wanted To Know About Real Estate Investing But Didn't Know Whom To Ask (Coming Soon!!!)
Author(s): *Anthony B. Miles and Renee D. Crenshaw*
Description: In this 200+ page real estate investing resource guide, Personal Finance Experts Renee D. Crenshaw and Anthony B. Miles provide tools, tips and hidden secrets to investing in urban real estate.
To reserve your copy: call (215) 222-0390

FUNDRAISING

Sponsorship Recruitment 101-102™ - A comprehensive self-help guide for parents, individuals and organizations seeking sponsorship!
Author(s): *Anthony B. Miles and Renee D. Crenshaw*
Description: Sponsorship Recruitment 101-102™ is an essential resource for parents, individuals and organizations worldwide. This 300+ page book developed by Anthony B. Miles and Renee D. Crenshaw transforms both new and experienced sponsorship seekers into "sponsorship pros" overnight. Join over 6,300 people throughout North America who have produce millions in FREE cash, products and services using Anthony's systematic approach.
Available: www.atlasbooks.com or 1-800-booklog

Sponsorship Recruitment 101-102™ - A one-day live interactive SPONSORSHIP INSTRUCTIONAL SEMINAR on DVD
Author(s): *Anthony B. Miles and Renee D. Crenshaw*
Description: Sponsorship Recruitment 101-102™ is an essential resource for parents, individuals and organizations worldwide. This one-day live interactive sponsorship instructional seminar on DVD presented by Anthony B. Miles and Renee D. Crenshaw transforms both new and experienced sponsorship seekers into "sponsorship pros" overnight. Join over 6,300 people throughout North America who have produce millions in FREE cash, products and services using Anthony's systematic approach.
Available: www.atlasbooks.com or 1-800-booklog

GLOSSARY OF TERMS

CREDIT GLOSSARY

Account number: Every account listed on your credit report should be listed by the account number. Never give out your credit card account number over the telephone unless you initiated the call and know to whom you are speaking.

Activate: To prevent fraud, many card issuers require you to call them when you receive your new card in the mail to verify that the correct person has received it. Until proper ownership is confirmed, the card may not be activated.

Activity: Activity is any transaction that appears on your bill, including purchases, cash advances, finance charges and fees. It also includes any payments made.

Additional cardmember/cardholder: Most issuers allow you to sign on an additional cardholder, such as a spouse, to your account. You are liable for any charges that the additional cardholder incurs.

Advance-fee loan: A loan calculated so that all the finance charges and other creditor expenses are deducted before the consumer receives the principal.

Agreement: Your card issuer will send you a cardholder agreement that describes the terms that apply to your card, including the interest rate charged, method of calculating interest and any transaction fees. If your card issuer refuses to disclose fully the terms of your card agreement before you accept the card, you might want to shop around for an issuer that will.

Amount due: Generally, the minimum monthly payment you must make, not the total amount you owe.

Annual fee: Card issuers may charge you a yearly fee in addition to the interest that accumulates when you make purchases. Depending on how you use it, a card with no annual fee but a high interest rate could cost you significantly more than one with a higher annual fee and a low, or no, interest rate.

Annual percentage rate (APR): The APR measures the cost of credit expressed as a yearly interest rate.

Automatic payment: If you have a savings or checking account with the same bank that issues your card, you may be able to automatically transfer money from your bank account to pay a credit card bill. Automatic payment eliminates the risk of paying a bill late and being assessed a late charge.

Available credit: The unused portion of credit that falls within the consumer's applicable credit limit, if any.

Average daily balance (including or excluding new purchases): The most common method of calculating interest. To figure out your average daily balance, the bank will add up the amount you owe for each day of your billing cycle and divide that number by the number of days in the billing cycle (see billing cycle). New purchases may or may not be added to the balance, depending on the individual card's terms. The most favorable calculation excludes new purchases.

Balance: Your balance is the amount of money you owe the card issuer, and includes purchases, fees, interest and transaction charges.

Bill aka monthly statement: Each billing cycle (usually once per month) your card issuer will send you a bill. The bill will detail the activity on your account for that billing cycle. The reverse side of your bill usually describes some of the basic terms of your card agreement, including how the interest is calculated and where to call with questions. See your card agreement for complete information on the terms.

Billing cycle: The time between your last bill and your current bill, usually 28 to 31 days.

Cash advance: You can use your card at a bank or an automatic teller machine to get a cash loan. The interest rate for a cash advance is typically higher than it is for purchases, and there is usually no grace period. There can also be a handling fee for withdrawing cash in addition to the interest charges, which can raise the cost significantly.

Charge card: A charge card requires you to pay your bill in full each month, but charges no interest.

Closing date: The closing date is the last day that transactions are posted on your account for that month.

Collateral: Savings, bonds, insurance policies, jewelry, property or other items that are pledged to pay off a loan or other debt if payments are not made according to the agreement. Also called security.

Collection agency: If you fail to pay a credit or charge card bill, the card issuer may send your overdue bill to a collection agency, a company that will attempt to obtain payment from you. If this happens, your account may be listed as a "collection account" on your credit report. If you do not pay your bill and your card issuer has to go to a collection agency to attempt to obtain payment from you, you may be liable for the cost of the collection agency's services. Check your cardholder agreement to see if your card includes this potential fee.

There are certain things a bill collector cannot lawfully **DO:** use or threaten to use violence or other criminal means to harm you, your property or your reputation; use obscene or profane language; publish your name; list your debt for sale to the public; or place telephone calls to you or any other person without identifying himself or herself as a bill collector. If a collection agency goes beyond these boundaries, you have legal rights protecting you.

Convenience check aka transfer check: When you open a new account with a credit card issuer, it may send you a blank convenience check or transfer check so you can shift the debt you have with your old card to your new card.

Copy charge aka document fee/charge: Card issuers are required to provide you with copies of documents relating to your account. They may, however, charge a fee for the copying and handling. See your cardholder agreement for your issuer's copy charges.

Co-sign: To sign a credit agreement with someone and agree to share the debt with that person or assume the debt if the other person defaults, that is, doesn't pay.

Co-signer: A parent or any person over 18 years old who agrees to share credit responsibilities and pay debts.

Credit bureau: A credit bureau keeps a record of your credit history for any card or loan issuer to review when considering your application for credit. The three major credit reporting agencies in the United States are Equifax, Experian (formerly TRW) and Trans Union.

Credit card: A credit card allows you to make partial payments for purchases, but charges interest on the amount owed. You can also pay your balance off in full to avoid interest payments. Banks and other card issuers set interest rates and fees.

Credit counseling: Advice given by professional counselors to people about how to use credit responsibly and how to get out of serious debt.

Credit limit: Your credit limit is the maximum amount you may charge on a credit card. Some card issuers set a separate limit for purchases and cash advances. Many banks will allow you to spend more than your credit limit, but may charge you a fee for doing so. It is up to you to keep track of your credit limit and how much available credit you have left.

Credit record/credit file: A person's up-to-date credit history.

Credit report: A summary of your recent credit history plus additional facts about you, including your age, address, marital status, employment history and other details that will help creditors judge your creditworthiness.

A credit report includes a record of any card that you hold now, held in the past, or for which you have applied. It also includes the credit limit and your payment history. You should request a copy of your credit report periodically to check it for accuracy. If you find an error, write to the credit bureau and request that the agency research and correct the error. You cannot have correct information removed from your records for seven years, or 10 years in the case of bankruptcy.

Credit union: A democratically owned and controlled nonprofit financial cooperative that offers a variety of savings and lending services to members.

Creditworthy: Judged to be qualified to have credit.

Daily periodic rate: The daily periodic rate is your annual interest rate expressed on a daily basis. It equals 1/365th of your annual percentage rate.

Debit card: This card allows you to deduct the amount of your purchase directly from your checking account for payment to the merchant.

Default: Failure to pay a debt as outlined in the cardholder agreement, bankruptcy, or an inability or unwillingness to pay your debt. If you default on your credit card account, the issuer will cancel your account and demand full payment of the outstanding balance.

Deferred payment: Payment put off to a future date or extended over a period of time. Watch out for skip-a-month offers. Interest still accumulates when you skip a month.

Delinquency assessment: A fee that is charged for a late payment.

Dispute: Credit and charge card bills are governed, in the United States, by the Fair Credit Billing Act, which is included in the Truth in Lending Act (see Truth in Lending Act) If you think your bill is wrong, write to your card issuer at the address listed on your statement. You must write no later than 60 days after receiving the first statement where the error appeared. The card issuer must acknowledge your letter within 30 days, and correct the error or explain why it thinks the statement was correct, within two billing cycles (but in no event later than 90 days) after receipt of your letter. You do not have to pay the amount in question while it is being investigated, but you must pay the rest of your bill.

Due date: The day a payment is due to a creditor. After that date, a late fee can be charged and the payment can be recorded as late, or the account can be considered delinquent.

Effective date: The first day your card is activated and ready for use or when new terms take effect.

Equal Credit Opportunity Act: The Equal Credit Opportunity Act requires that U.S. financial institutions and other creditors make credit equally available to all creditworthy customers without regard to race, color, religion, national origin, sex, marital status or age. For example, a creditor cannot ask you to reapply, close your account or change terms of a loan if you become widowed or divorced. Income from pensions, annuities or part-time employment may not be excluded by a creditor in evaluating a consumer's creditworthiness.

Fair Credit Billing Act: See dispute.

Fair Credit Reporting Act: The U.S. Fair Credit Reporting Act seeks to achieve fair, timely and accurate reporting of credit information by regulating the activities of credit bureaus, limiting access to credit bureau information, and requiring that creditors disclose certain information regarding their use of credit bureau or third party information. Under the Fair Credit Reporting Act, you have the right to see the credit history maintained by a credit bureau about you (see credit report).

Federal Reserve: A central bank that monitors and influences the total supply of money and credit through its 12 regional offices. The Federal Reserve Board sets interest rates, maintains the flow of cash to local and regional banks, clears checks, provides deposit insurance, and helps guarantee the stability and security of the U.S. banking system.

Finance charge: The cost of consumer credit expressed as a dollar amount. A finance charge would include the following types of charges imposed by card issuers: interest, transaction fees and service fees.

Finance company: A business that makes consumer loans, often to consumers who cannot qualify for credit at a credit union or bank. Typically, the interest rates charged by a finance company are higher than those charged by other creditors.

Goods and services dispute: If you have a problem with the quality of property or services that you purchase with a charge or credit card, and you have tried in good faith to correct the problem with the merchant, you may have the right not to pay the remaining amount due on the property or services. There are two limitations on this right: 1) You must have made the purchase in your home state or, if not within your home state, within 100 miles of your current mailing address, and 2) the purchase price must have been more than $50.

Grace period: The period of time, generally 20 to 25 days, from the billing date of your last credit card bill to the due date of your current bill, when you can pay in full without being charged interest. Some cards do not offer a grace period. Others only have a grace period if there was no outstanding balance on the account at the start of the billing cycle. Generally, there is no grace period for cash advances.

Inquiry: Your credit report has an inquiry section that lists anyone who has asked for your credit history.

Installment credit: A credit agreement that allows you to repay credit in regular payments over a specified time.

Interest: A charge for borrowed money, generally a percentage of the amount owed.

Joint account: Two people can share a card, each individually responsible for the outstanding balance on the card account. (This is different from having one person apply as a cardholder, with additional cards on that account issued to family members or others. For more information, see additional cardmember/cardholder.)

Late payment: Most charge and credit card bills list the date by which payments are due. If you miss the due date, the account is considered past due and you may be charged a fee. Your credit report may reflect late payments, and if you have made a habit of paying late, creditors may be dissuaded from granting additional credit.

Liability: Liability refers to the responsibility for charges to an account. Generally, a cardholder agrees to be liable for any charges to his or her account, including purchases, fees and finance charges. If the cardholder allows someone else to make charges to his or her account (through, for example, an additional card), the cardholder is still responsible for paying the bill. Two people who apply for a card together may both be responsible for the entire balance. Your liability is described in the cardholder agreement you receive from the issuer. Be sure to read it carefully.

Minimum payment: The minimum amount you are required to pay the credit card issuer each month. You may, however, choose to pay more. Paying the minimum monthly payment may be helpful when you can only afford to make a small payment. However, interest charges can really add up when you stretch out a loan with minimum payments.

For example, at an 18.5 percent interest rate, it will take you more than 11 years to pay off a debt of $2,000 if you only pay the minimum balance due each month. During this time, you will pay interest charges of $1,934 — almost doubling the cost of your purchase. (This calculation is based on making a payment which is 1/36th of the outstanding balance, or $20, whichever is larger.)

Monthly periodic rate: The rate of interest per month, calculated by dividing the annual percentage rate (APR) by 12.

Other charges: Other charges may be listed on your bill and can include the annual membership fee or late payment fees.

Over-the-limit fee: When you charge more than your credit limit allows, you may be charged an over-the-limit, or over-credit-limit, fee. Your card issuer may allow you to exceed your credit limit without telling you in advance, and you may not know you have done so until you receive your bill.

Overdraft agreement: Some issuers allow you to link your credit card to a checking or savings account that you hold with that bank. When you sign an overdraft agreement and you bounce a check, the bank can charge that amount to your credit card account and the check will clear. This way, you avoid a returned-check fee.

Partial payment: Paying less than the full amount due.

Past due: When you do not make at least the minimum payment on time, your account is considered past due.

Periodic rate: The interest rate described in relation to a specific amount of time. For example, the monthly periodic rate is the cost of credit per month; the daily periodic rate is the cost of credit per day.

Posting date: The date that a transaction is recorded on your account. Some companies assess interest on charges and cash advances from the transaction date (see transaction date), others from the posting date. It is more favorable to assess interest from the posting date, because that may be later, giving you some interest-free days.

Previous balance: The amount you still owe after last month's payments and charges were added to your balance.

Prime rate: The interest rate banks charge for loans to their biggest and highest-rated customers. The prime rate changes based on the demand for money and the rate the U.S. Federal Reserve Bank charges to its member banks. It is used as a major economic indicator.

Principal: The amount of money you owe, not including the interest due on it.

Promotional aka introductory rate: An interest rate that applies for a limited amount of time. After the time limit expires, the ongoing rate (which is usually higher) is applied to your outstanding balance. Check both rates when deciding which card offers the most value.

Rebate/enhancement cards: Some cards include rebates on merchandise or cash-back offers depending on how much you charge annually. Others have enhancements that offer special benefits, such as frequent-flier miles or long-distance telephone discounts. When choosing a rebate card, be sure that the rebates the card provides add up to more than what you might save with a lower interest rate card.

Revolve: To carry over a debt from month to month, paying interest on the amount owed.

Revolving credit: A credit agreement that allows consumers to pay all or part of the outstanding balance on a loan or credit card. As credit is paid off, it becomes available again to use for another purchase or cash advance.

Secured credit card or loan: A consumer uses savings or other collateral to guarantee the credit card or loan; the limit of credit is based on the amount of collateral available.

SET protocol: Secure electronic transaction protocol, an encryption technology designed to allow secure electronic transactions between card issuers, merchants and consumers. Unsecured information sent over the Internet can be intercepted. When making purchases online, you should consider a secure browser that complies with industry standards, such as secure sockets layer (SSL) or secure hypertext transfer protocol (S-HTTP). These often are included with Internet connection services.

Smart card: A card containing a central processing unit (CPU) that stores and secures information and makes decisions, as required by the card issuer's specific application needs.

Status: A credit report will describe the status of your accounts — the type of account (charge, credit or installment loan) and whether your account has been paid on time, is past due or canceled.

Stored value card: An information storage card that contains stored value, which the user can "spend" in a pay phone, retail, vending or related transaction.

Transaction date: The date a purchase is made or cash is withdrawn. Some companies assess interest on charges and cash advances from the transaction date, others from the posting date (see posting date).

Transaction fee: A fee that is charged each time certain transactions take place, for example, cash advances.

Truth in Lending Act: The Truth in Lending Act seeks to tell U.S. consumers important information about credit terms that can help them make informed credit choices and should protect them against inaccurate and unfair billing practices. The Truth in Lending Act was amended by, and includes, the Fair Credit Billing Act (see dispute).

Unsecured loan: A loan based on a consumer's promise to pay, without savings or other collateral as a guarantee. Sometimes called a signature loan.

Unused credit: The amount of credit you have available before you reach your credit limit.

Variable interest rate: A variable interest rate is based on fluctuating rates in the banking system, such as the prime rate. For example, if on January 1, the prime rate was 6 percent and your credit card's variable rate formula was the prime rate plus 9.9 percent, your interest rate would be 15.9 percent (see prime rates).

Zero balance: If you have no previous outstanding balances on your card account and no new activity that month, this means that you have a zero balance. You might not get a bill since you do not owe anything.

INDEX

CREDIT INDEX

D

ADDITIONAL ORDERS

Telephone: Call 1-800-booklog toll free. Have your credit card handy.

E-mail: orders@bookmasters.com

Web: www.atlasbooks.com

ATTENTION CORPORATIONS, CHURCHES, SCHOOLS AND NONPROFIT ORGANIZATIONS

Everything You Wanted To Know About Credit is available at quantity discounts with bulk purchase for educational, business, or sales promotional use. For more information, please write Rising Star Foundation Special Sales, 643 N. 33rd Street, 1st floor, Philadelphia, PA 19104. Please supply title of the book, quantity, how the book will be used and date needed.

Phone: (215) 222-0390

NOTES

NOTES

NOTES

NOTES